PRAISE FOR *HELPING WITHOU* *SHORT-TERM MISSIO*

Our world is rapidly changing, even in the way we do Christ-exalting missions! In this helpful book, the Chalmers Center has given us an insightful resource that will equip short-term mission teams to avoid pitfalls of crossing cultures, especially for those embarking on communities challenged by poverty. Teams will build their capacity to learn well, honor partnerships, and maximize the good they wish to do by using this guidebook to help design their objectives with faithful presence, understanding, and humility.

John H. Sather | National Director of Cru Inner City

This [curriculum] takes the best of the revolutionary work from *When Helping Hurts* and makes it practical for short-term mission teams traveling near and far. I highly commend this resource to you as a way to serve with cultural intelligence.

David Livermore, PhD | Author of *Serving with Eyes Wide Open: Doing Short-Term Missions with Cultural Intelligence*

Being a community development organization that has sent thousands of people on short-term trips to developing countries over the years, we are thrilled to introduce Fikkert and Corbett's latest work as a relevant, vital resource for our staff and teams. It is our strong desire that every church, school, and NGO sending (or receiving) short-term teams would not only read this book, but study it—critically evaluating the work being accomplished and applying its principles to ensure teams are "helping without hurting."

Kurt Kandler | Executive Director of The 410 Bridge

If everyone responsible for sending *or* receiving a short-term service team can work through this resource—and take seriously its recommendations—I have no doubt that we will see the fruit in changed lives and stronger relationships within the global church.

Brian Howell, PhD | Professor of Anthropology at Wheaton College, author of *Short-Term Mission: An Ethnography of Christian Travel Narrative and Experience*

Helping Without Hurting in Short-Term Missions is one of the most useful guides on STM in print. . . . [*When Helping Hurts*] shaped the way compassionate people should think about engaging the materially poor. This book guides the way for short-term missioners to accompany the poor in real and lasting transformation.

Daniel Rickett, PhD | Cofounder of Coalition on the Support of Indigenous Ministries, author of *Making Your Partnership Work*

There is no shortcut to living the incarnation among others in another culture. Anyone serious about truly helping will immediately see the value of this book and be grateful to put it to good use.

Scott Steele | Executive Director at Cherokee Gives Back Foundation

These principles will help the church move beyond good intentions and toward a discipleship model that equips team members to become lifelong missionaries wherever they are, encourages partnership with local churches globally, and truly helps advance the work of God globally.

Jeff Ward | Director of External Focus at Watermark Community Church

What really sells me on these materials is that they address what to me is the #1 question for STM participants: How do we make sure the two-week mission experience turns into a long-term commitment both to the project we visited and to serving in the communities where we live?

Kurt Ver Beek, PhD | Professor of Sociology at Calvin College

Finally, a short-term missions curriculum that gets it right! For too long church leaders have known something is wrong with the way the church does short-term missions, but not how to fix it. This book will change that. It starts with an honest appraisal of the mistakes we've been making but moves on to provide smart, practical tools to transform the way we do short-term missions. A must-read for any group that wants to do short-term missions right. Two thumbs way up!

Jo Ann Van Engen | Codirector, Semester in Honduras, Calvin College

Our short-term mission culture warrants major rethinking. This book is a priceless tool because it helps do just that, providing an alternative paradigm for cross-cultural engagement and a framework for the "messy" process of reform.

Tim Ritter | Discipleship Coordinator at Reality SF

Yes, yes, yes! This book could change the way we do missions. Every chapter is right on target, delineating the costs and complexity of a trip, and demonstrating how to make it part of long-term engagement.

Miriam Adeney, PhD | Associate Professor of Global and Urban Ministry at Seattle Pacific University, author of *Kingdom Without Borders: The Untold Story of Global Christianity*

This book challenges stewardship of our finances, encourages accountability, and acknowledges that cross-cultural interaction is an incredible process when done with plenty of grace.

McKenna Raasch | Director of Global Outreach at Calvary Church, Los Gatos

Almost no one has helped shape how our church thinks about global poverty as much as Brian Fikkert and Steve Corbett. This book furthers the discussion about effective gospel-based poverty relief strategies by translating the grand, compelling vision of *When Helping Hurts* into clear, actionable steps for churches. Our missions team has read this book, and we are implementing many of the insights within it.

J.D. Greear, PhD | author, *Gospel: Recovering the Power That Made Christianity Revolutionary* and *Breaking the Islam Code*

HELPING WITHOUT HURTING

IN SHORT-TERM MISSIONS

• • •

Leader's Guide

STEVE CORBETT
and BRIAN FIKKERT

MOODY PUBLISHERS

CHICAGO

© 2014 by
STEVE CORBETT AND BRIAN FIKKERT

All rights reserved. No part of this book may be reproduced in any form without permission in writing from the publisher, except in the case of brief quotations embodied in critical articles or reviews.

Scripture quotations are taken from the Holy Bible, New International Version®, NIV®. Copyright © 1973, 1978, 1984, 2011 by Biblica, Inc.™ Used by permission of Zondervan. All rights reserved worldwide. www.zondervan.com. The "NIV" and "New International Version" are trademarks registered in the United States Patent and Trademark Office by Biblica, Inc.™

Crafted for the Chalmers Center by Katie Casselberry
Moody Publishers editor: Pam Pugh
Cover design: Faceout Studio
Cover image: Crocodile Images/Thinkstock
Interior design: Smartt Guys design

Library of Congress Cataloging-in-Publication Data
Corbett, Steve.
  Helping without hurting in short-term missions : leader's guide / Steve Corbett and Brian Fikkert.
    pages cm
  Includes bibliographical references.
  ISBN 978-0-8024-1229-4
  1. Short-term missions--Study and teaching. I. Title.
  BV2082.S56C67 2014
  266--dc23
                                2014018802

All websites and phone numbers listed herein are accurate at the time of publication but may change in the future or cease to exist. The listing of website references and resources does not imply publisher endorsement of the site's entire contents. Groups and organizations are listed for informational purposes, and listing does not imply publisher endorsement of their activities.

We hope you enjoy this book from Moody Publishers. Our goal is to provide high-quality, thought-provoking books and products that connect truth to your real needs and challenges. For more information on other books and products written and produced from a biblical perspective, go to www.moodypublishers.com or write to:

Moody Publishers
820 N. LaSalle Boulevard
Chicago, IL 60610

5 7 9 10 8 6 4

Printed in the United States of America

CONTENTS

PARTICIPANT'S GUIDE WITH SCRIPTING

INTRODUCTION—THE NEED FOR THIS GUIDE

During my (Steve's) time working with a Christian relief and development organization, I had the opportunity to see short-term mission trips up close and personal. One team was particularly memorable. The group, made up of mostly adults, came with such a spirit of humility. They came with open minds and hearts, wanting to better understand poverty and poverty alleviation in the South American region in which we worked. They visited and stayed in several communities. They met with national field staff, pastors, teachers, committee leaders, and community members. They attended church events and were full participants in them, but they did not feel the need to lead, teach, or preach. In fact, they politely declined invitations to do so, deferring to the leadership of local pastors. They came to simply *be* with us.

I personally knew some of the trip participants, and I had a chance to follow up with their stories. Even as they returned home, they stood with their brothers and sisters on the field. Most of them became dedicated advocates for the work we were doing, and they supported our work through their financial generosity. They unleashed our local staff to engage in transformational work that simply couldn't have happened otherwise. Their trip was a huge success. Thinking of my time with them still puts a smile on my face.

WHY ANOTHER RESOURCE?

In terms of the number of pages and words, there is no shortage of resources for short-term mission trips (STMs). A simple Internet search uncovers countless leader's guides, activity suggestions, and procedural checklists for both participants and team leaders. In light of such a mountain of information, it may seem pointless to dedicate yet *more* ink to STMs.

Then why create another STM resource? Short-term missions, as often practiced today, need a reformation. They need a healthier vision and practical framework in order to be more effective. Some trips, like the one I described above, lead to deep, transformative work on the field and in participants' attitudes and actions. But I also know of stories where teams constructed buildings one week and local people tore them down the next week, ensuring that subsequent groups had some work to do. I know of stories where the same local people came forward to be baptized week after week so that teams felt like their evangelism efforts were effective. These are obviously extreme scenarios, and clearly the sending churches did not intend to create these situations. But such stories represent one end of the STM spectrum. We hope this guide can contribute to moving churches—wherever they are on the continuum—toward a healthier approach to short-term trips.

However, the ideas in this guide are not completely new. Countless missiologists, sociologists, and church and ministry leaders have written about the need for a revised approach to STMs, providing suggestions for how that approach might become a reality. Several organizations have even compiled documents describing best practices for trips, including the Standards of Excellence in Short-Term Mission.[1] By emphasizing elements like pre-trip training, healthy partnerships, and intentional follow-up, these leaders have outlined what effective STMs look like. But seemingly few materials exist that channel this research into a concrete resource for churches and ministries to use with their teams when entering low-income communities. *Helping Without Hurting in Short-Term Missions* is designed to help bridge that gap for both leaders and participants.

DEFINING OUR TERMS

Rather than focusing on the trip itself as the defining element of a short-term experience, this guide situates short-term visits as one piece in a larger undertaking. A trip is not, in and of itself, typically a catalyst for change in a community—or enough to move team members toward meaningful participation in poverty alleviation. Thus, while the following pages talk about pre- and post-trip activities, it is important to remember that the goal is learning about, engaging in, and supporting poverty alleviation and missions. The definition of a "healthy" trip includes long-term engagement and learning.

Further, this guide defines "short-term" as trips of approximately seven to fourteen days. Such a narrow definition is not intended to ignore the existence of six-month, one-year, or multi-year commitments. Rather, for the sake of clarity, this project is deliberately addressing trips as they most frequently exist in sending churches.

WHAT IS SUCCESS?

On one level, success for this guide means that churches are no longer, through their STMs, inflicting inadvertent harm on communities that are materially poor. It also means challenging misunderstandings about the appropriate and realistic purposes of trips, focusing on a long-term process of learning and engagement rather than executing particular tasks.

On another level, we believe that part of improving short-term trips actually involves taking fewer of them, dedicating more of our resources to long-term missions and poverty alleviation work within a community. Thus, success for this guide will be measured by more and more churches and believers engaging with, praying for, and supporting effective ministries and their staff, missionaries, or community development workers. It means more and more churches turning loose their brothers and sisters who work in low-income communities every day, supporting them as they do work that outsiders could never accomplish in two weeks. In that sense, a congregation that is supporting local workers without creating dependency, even without recurring short-term trips, is one of the biggest long-term successes that could come from this project.

The shift toward long-term work involves another facet of success. The process of moving churches toward long-term engagement both requires and creates a deeper understanding of effective poverty alleviation approaches. It fosters an appreciation for diversity and differences in culture. It instills a deep respect for the body of Christ across miles and languages. And it develops humility in comparably affluent churches and individuals as we recognize the way *all* of us are dependent on the healing work of Jesus Christ in our lives.

Thus, this guide is also designed as a discipleship tool for church leaders to use with participants. Again, when done well, a short-term trip itself is just one piece of the broader, long-term journey of learning and engagement with God's work in the world. Leading participants through that process can be a powerful piece of helping them understand—and advocate within their congregations for—redefining poverty and poverty alleviation in their own communities. Through this type of transformation, both sending churches and churches across the globe can better share the gospel in word and deed. Ultimately, there is no greater success than the local body of Christ declaring and demonstrating the hope of Jesus Christ's reconciling work.

WHAT THIS GUIDE IS—AND ISN'T

Be aware that this guide is written for short-term teams entering low-income contexts, particularly those where poverty alleviation is being attempted. It is not designed to prepare a team for street evangelism in London or Chicago. While some of the general principles could apply to having STMs visit communities that do not experience extensive poverty, it is not a generic STM resource.

Within the general context of two-week trips, the following chapters articulate a more positive way of engaging with low-income communities. Incorporating the principles of effective poverty alleviation described in *When Helping Hurts*, this project addresses the elements of STMs that need to be refined in order to avoid harming low-income communities, to effect change in participants' understanding of poverty alleviation, and to foster increased support for long-term missions and development work.

Because this guide is focused on shifting the fundamental way we approach trips, it is not an all-encompassing toolbox for running an STM program. We are not including packing lists, instructions for obtaining visas, or suggestions for managing emergency contact information.

NAVIGATING ENDLESS POSSIBILITIES

One of the challenges in making a resource like this practical is the countless variables in trips—even in two-week trips to communities that experience poverty. For example, the process of sending a short-term team through a direct congregation-to-congregation relationship takes different types of planning than partnering through an intermediary organization. Going with a large third-party organization that is doing quality poverty alleviation work provides enormous benefits to you and the receiving community. These organizations should have existing country- or region-specific training resources, and they can mediate your relationship with local churches and community members. However, engaging in direct congregation-to-congregation relationships can be very rewarding when done well, though they take increased investment of human and financial resources, time, and energy.

For the sake of clarity, this guide addresses two basic forms of trips:

- **Lay learning trips**: Trips focused on offering congregation members a chance to see, engage with, and more deeply understand what poverty is, what quality poverty alleviation looks like, and what the implications are for their lives.

- **Strategic partnership trips**: Trips with a smaller group of church leaders that serve a strategic purpose, such as exploring, developing, or assessing long-term collaboration.

These two types of trips should complement each other, and the general concepts in this guide apply to both. However, because the most common short-term trips are focused on broader church participation, this guide is primarily tailored to the experiences of lay learning trips. Chapter 5 will unpack a few ideas about strategic partnership trips, but they are not the primary focus of this resource.

Healthy short-term trips will also vary based on a host of contextual factors. A trip to a community in the Majority World (Africa, Asia, or Latin America) will look different from trips in a US context, just as the dynamics of a trip with teens will differ from the dynamics present with a group of adults. While the principles in this book, such as the importance of distinguishing among relief, rehabilitation, and development, apply to all trips, they will take on additional nuances when applied to some specialized trips. Medical mission trips, for example, may provide a service that is completely unavailable in a particular community, adding more complexity to respecting the difference between relief and development.

With this many variables and moving parts, it is impossible to create step-by-step guidelines for every conceivable type of trip. Thus, different kinds of trips present different challenges and levels of work. Be aware that this guide cannot walk through every possible scenario.

However, one piece is common to any healthy short-term trip: wherever the team goes, they are sent to support an organization or ministry that is engaging in effective poverty alleviation. Situating a short-term trip in the context of an organization's long-term work helps prevent certain types of inadvertent harm. Further, it can lead churches into deep, lasting engagement with effective work in your own community and around the world.

HOW TO USE THESE MATERIALS

This resource assumes that you, as the leader of the short-term trip, have read *When Helping Hurts* and are familiar with its basic concepts. Throughout the text, references will be provided to the relevant chapters of *When Helping Hurts*.

The *Leader's Guide* is structured to address basic principles and context for healthy trips (chapters 1–3) and the implementation of trips from this alternative framework (chapters 4–9). The *Participant's Guide* and the corresponding video units are designed to shepherd participants through the preparatory, on-field, and follow-up stages of the trip, increasing their understanding of poverty alleviation and ways for them to contribute to such work.

For simplicity's sake, the *Participant's Guide* is printed in the back of this volume with a separate introduction and some annotations for you to reference as you facilitate each session.

Moving toward a more effective approach to short-term trips can be a messy, sometimes demoralizing, process. But it is also incredibly rewarding. As you begin rethinking your short-term trips, remember that the Holy Spirit is the ultimate author of change. God is at work in the world, in your heart, and in your church. And we have the responsibility and privilege of being an active participant in that process, seeking to intentionally come alongside His work.

Hopefully this guide can be a blessing in that journey of engagement and transformation, moving your church forward in helping without hurting in short-term missions. But we, as authors, also see this resource as a living project. Thus, we invite you to speak into it as you use it. Let us know what worked well or did not work well with your teams. Share encouraging stories from your groups and suggestions for improvement. Send feedback to stm@chalmers.org.

Thank you for embracing both the beauty and challenges of doing short-term trips well. May the God of grace, perseverance, and wisdom guide you, your team, and your church.

TAKEAWAYS

- Be open to speaking into this resource, becoming a part of a learning community seeking to improve STMs to low-income areas.

- For general context, review chapter 7 of *When Helping Hurts* before going any farther.

SUGGESTED LEARNING SEQUENCING

This table is not meant to be a list of all material that will need to be covered in pre-trip preparation; obviously a host of logistical questions will require time, discussion, and meetings. It is merely an attempt to order the specific learning components described in the Leader's Guide.

Orientation/Informational Meeting: Preview "Learning and Engagement Agreement"
Fundraising: See resource module A. The ideas this module addresses will make more sense to the participants after completing unit 4. However, that point in the process will probably be too late for most people to begin raising support. Decide when to have participants utilize the counsel in module A given your context and timeframe.
Unit 1
Unit 2
Unit 3
Unit 4
Community-Specific Context Discussion: History, economics, church history, etc.
Unit 5
Community-Specific Cultural Training: See resource module B for cultural norm summaries.
Unit 6 (On-Field)
Unit 7: May require an extended session.
Unit 8
Ongoing Accountability Meetings: monthly or bimonthly basis
Additional sessions throughout: Add to this sequencing other meetings you need to make sure the team is fully prepared for the trip and processes the experience well.

PART ONE

. . .

A DIFFERENT
SORT OF TRIP

CHAPTER 1

MISSION ACCOMPLISHED?

UNCOMFORTABLE QUESTIONS AND STMs

They stream through the airport, backpacks and matching shirts bobbing through security lines, and then sleepily relax at the gates. They pile into vans, pillows and trail mix crammed between every seat. There were 120,000 in 1989; 450,000 in 1998; 1,000,000 in 2003; and 2,200,000 in 2006. The numbers reflect a tidal wave of American short-term "missionaries" flooding the world.[1]

And the movement continues to grow.[2] Research from 2010 suggests that the number of people from the US traveling on international STMs each year has likely risen to 2–3 million.[3] To look at it from a different angle, Robert Wuthnow, professor of sociology at Princeton University, estimates that the likelihood of any given US church member going on an international STM sometime in their lifetime could be as high as 20–25 percent.[4]

But STMs as we think of them today are a recent phenomenon. Sixty years ago, traveling from Iowa to Kenya required an enormous financial and time investment. Now, high school students from Seattle can afford a plane ticket to visit South Africa for two weeks—and they can make the trip year after year, easily raising funds each summer.

This is a gift. The world has shrunk remarkably in the space of a few decades, creating new opportunities to engage with the body of Christ and see the work God is doing through His people. The apostle Paul spent his life sailing around the Mediterranean world visiting churches, often arriving shipwrecked, waterlogged, or snakebitten. Now we can hop on an Airbus and arrive halfway across the world ten hours later, rarely experiencing anything worse than a bit of turbulence and jetlag. Early believers, or even the missionaries of 150 years ago, could never have dreamed of such an opportunity.

But the rise of STMs has left church leaders, missionaries, and organizations on both the sending and receiving side of the STM equation asking important questions: How well are we stewarding this opportunity and the resources God has entrusted to us? How do we do STMs well? What are the potential positive and negative effects of STMs? How can we shepherd participants in meaningful transformation and learning through these trips? How can we ensure our STMs are not harming the materially poor? These are weighty questions, and they require honest reflection by church leaders and congregation members.

It is exciting to see churches wrestling with the place of short-term missions in the life of the body of Christ. But this conversation has a context. How STMs began and how they became known as "missions" should inform where we go from here.

NOT MERELY SEMANTICS[5]

At the end of the nineteenth century, the word "missionary" described someone who packed up a few meager belongings, sometimes in the coffin they planned to be buried in, and permanently said goodbye to their families. They then sailed for an unknown region of the world, spending their lives sharing the gospel with people who had never heard of Jesus Christ. Of course, the missionary movement was not perfect. "Conversion" to Christianity was sometimes associated with political and cultural domination, not just proclaiming the gospel and partaking in equal fellowship in the body of Christ. But one thing was certain: being a missionary meant sacrifice. And it meant long-term permanent commitment. It was not until the 1950s and 1960s that the idea of a short-term presence on the mission field grew in popularity, largely thanks to the development of cheaper and faster travel. And even then, short-term work typically lasted several months and was seen primarily as an opportunity to recruit lifelong missionaries. These short-term experiences were not frequently labeled as "mission," a word reserved for long-term work.

Throughout the 1970s and 1980s, more and more people, including students and youth who had no direct interest in becoming long-term workers, began taking short-term trips. As a result, trips were increasingly framed as opportunities for personal growth in addition to local service and impact.[6] The label of "missionary" was gradually applied to short-term participants, in spite of this heavy emphasis on personal transformation. But even in the early 1990s, there were still many theologians and missionaries who were uncomfortable using the same word, "mission," to describe both a two-week trip and a twenty-year commitment.

Nonetheless, by the start of the twenty-first century, the phrase "short-term mission trip" was cemented in the popular vocabulary of many evangelical churches. However, the typical structure and purpose of these trips is still shifting. Between language barriers and cultural differences, many churches are realizing that STMs are not always conducive to evangelism and discipleship efforts. As a result, there has been an increase in the number of STMs focused specifically on poverty alleviation—an endeavor that seems manageable and concrete in the space of the typical two-week trip.[7]

Many churches are not even aware that the rise of short-term trips as mission was a controversial process, or that the definition of STM is constantly evolving. But this nuanced history should inform the way we use the word "mission" today. We need to use it carefully, for when we speak it we are invoking nothing less than God's purposes and His work in the world—not simply a brand of program or service project to be constantly adapted to the latest trends. How does the work of our short-term teams fit into God's overarching mission? Are our current trips self-consciously and introspectively submitting to His goals, not just in theory and language, but in practice?

THE MISSION OF GOD

Answering these questions requires us to step back and ask, "What exactly is God's mission in the world?" Christians often answer this question in slightly different ways. Some say that God's mission is to glorify Himself. Others say it is to save people from their sins. Still others say it is to serve the poor and oppressed.

This guide is not intended to be a missiological treatise. But for the sake of clarity, we will talk about the mission of God in the terms of Colossians 1: God is reconciling all things to Himself through the blood of Jesus Christ shed on the cross.

> For he has rescued us from the dominion of darkness and brought us into the kingdom of the Son he loves, in whom we have redemption, the forgiveness of sins. The Son is the image of the invisible God, the firstborn over all creation. For in him all things were created: things in heaven and on earth, visible and invisible, whether thrones or powers or rulers or authorities; all things have been created through him and for him. He is before all things, and in him all things hold together. And he is the head of the body, the church; he is the beginning and the firstborn from among the dead, so that in everything he might have the supremacy. For God was pleased to have all his fullness dwell in him, and through him to reconcile to himself all things, whether things on earth or things in heaven, by making peace through his blood, shed on the cross.

—COLOSSIANS 1:13–20

God created the universe and called it "good," but sin marred His original design. Rather than leaving the creation to ruin, Colossians 1 teaches that God's mission is to reconcile all things, meaning that He is restoring His creation to the fullness of what He intended it to be. This restoration is comprehensive in scope, transforming individuals, communities, nature, cultures, institutions, and systems. It all matters, because Christ is the creator, sustainer, and reconciler of all of it.

However, the full benefits of this restoration are only for those who repent of their sins and put their faith in Jesus Christ and His atoning sacrifice, while judgment awaits those who do not. These truths should give us incredible passion to communicate—in both words and deeds—the gospel in all its fullness, for God's mission is truly good news for those who believe. (See chapters 1 and 2 of *When Helping Hurts* for a review of these themes.)

UNDERSTANDING POVERTY

Throughout the Old and New Testaments, God shows a particular concern that His mission of comprehensive reconciliation touch the lives of materially poor people in ways that restore them to all that it means to be image-bearers. Among other things, this means restoring poor people to being able to work and to support themselves and their families through that work. This is more easily said than done, for the root causes of poverty are difficult to diagnose and treat.

Many churches and short-term trips that focus on poverty alleviation tend to think that poverty is primarily about a lack of material things such as food, clothing, and shelter. As a result, they tend to focus their efforts on providing these material things to low-income people. In contrast to this common view of poverty, low-income people tend to describe their poverty in far more psychological and social terms, often expressing a profound sense of shame, inferiority, helplessness, vulnerability, and social isolation. This disconnect between how we think of poverty and how the poor actually experience poverty is at the heart of the crisis in poverty alleviation efforts. We need a sound diagnosis of the underlying disease of poverty if we are to apply the proper treatment.

From a biblical perspective, poverty is rooted in broken relationships with God, self, others, and the rest of creation. In this light, material poverty is a symptom of something deeper. We need to stop treating the symptoms and start treating the underlying causes of poverty; indeed, treating the symptoms, e.g., continually giving handouts of material resources, can actually make matters worse by undermining the materially poor's dignity and stewardship. We need to see poverty alleviation as a process of reconciling both the materially poor and non-poor to right relationship with God, self, others, and the rest of creation. In other words, poverty alleviation is about participating in the reconciling mission of God expressed in Colossians 1. (See chapters 2 and 3 of *When Helping Hurts* for a recap of these ideas.)

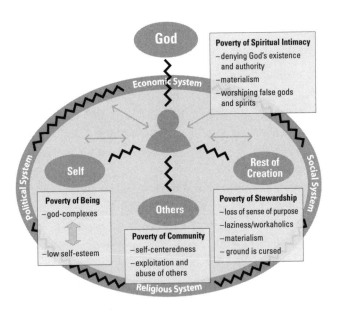

Adapted from Bryant L. Myers, *Walking with the Poor: Principles and Practices of Transformational Development* (Maryknoll, NY: Orbis Books, 1999), 27.

Here's the uncomfortable truth: *because poverty alleviation is a long-term process of reconciliation, not a momentary provision of material goods, a standalone, two-week STM trip cannot significantly and directly contribute to poverty alleviation. But the trip can make poverty worse!* Please go back and read that previous sentence again, for it is one of the central messages of this book.

The growing emphasis on STMs that engage in poverty alleviation is rooted in a flawed understanding of what poverty actually is and of what poverty alleviation actually entails. *It is not just a material problem that can be addressed through providing material resources on two-week trips.*

The cosmic scope of both the brokenness of the fall and the power of Christ's redemptive work has to frame the way we plan, speak about, and evaluate STM efforts in materially poor communities. There *is* a way to do STMs that supports the long-term work God is already doing in a community, that avoids hurting those we are trying to help, and that leads to transformative engagement. But first we have to evaluate the current balance sheet of STMs—including the commonly cited benefits of these trips.

BENEFIT PACKAGES

When church members describe the perceived benefits and impact of STMs on participants, several themes quickly emerge: *STM participants give more to long-term missions. They are more involved in ministry in their communities. They are more thankful for what God has given them. They form long-term relationships with low-income people. They may even become life-long missionaries.* Incredible things do happen through STMs. Participating in an STM has changed many people's lives, and that is a beautiful thing that we should never dismiss.

Unfortunately, within the body of quantitative research dedicated to the impact of STMs on participants, many studies rely on self-reported data from team members soon after their return from the trip. Very few studies follow up with participants a year or more after the experience, and even fewer corroborate self-reported data by studying participants' actual behaviors. The very limited research available that does dig into longer-term behavioral change in participants suggests that lasting personal transformation as a result of STMs is relatively low in percentage terms.

For example, Kurt Ver Beek, professor of sociology at Calvin College with more than twenty years of experience in Honduras, has conducted research into the long-term impact of the STM trips on team members, looking beyond their initial statements to their actual behaviors. Ver Beek's data indicate that there is not a significant increase in participants' long-term missions giving to either the receiving organization or their sending churches.[8] And as for all the relationships that develop during STMs, the reality is that only a small percentage of STM team members ever have any contact with their new "friends" after the trip ends. It is also hard to support the claim that STMs directly and independently increase the number of long-term missionaries, given that the number of long-term missionaries over the past fifteen years is fairly stable despite the explosion of STM trips.[9, 10]

Sociologist LiErin Probasco adds to this discussion by surveying the long-term impact of participating in an STM as a teen. She found that participation in an international STM as a teen has no significant impact on either giving or volunteering behaviors in the adults studied. She also found that participants in domestic trips did not exhibit increased financial support for their local congregations. However, domestic participants were more likely to volunteer their time toward work in their own community and abroad.[11] Reflecting on this data, Probasco suggests that the "novelty, intensity, and 'shock'" of international trips could actually hinder participants from translating and applying their experiences to their own contexts, undermining their likelihood to engage over the long haul.[12] While there is more research to be done in this area, her initial observations should make us consider the way we think about and market the impact of STMs. Our focus on crafting extreme and stretching experiences to create change might actually be setting up barriers to lasting transformation and action in participants' lives.

Although there is a need for many more studies, the current research should give us pause about the extent to which STMs as often currently practiced are catalysts for widespread and lasting personal change. For some people, they are incredibly transformative, and we should always recognize and rejoice in that transformation. But given the scale of STMs in our churches, we must also consider how we can make such positive outcomes more frequent, and we certainly should not claim that STM involvement automatically or consistently leads to transformation.

Similar claims of positive change are made about the impact of STMs on low-income communities: *STM teams build houses and provide clean water that wouldn't exist any other way. They lead people to salvation. They show children love that they would have never received otherwise.* Unfortunately, there is a lack of systematic research focused on the effect of STMs on receiving communities experiencing material poverty. However, some practitioners and researchers are questioning whether there is as much of a lasting positive impact as the teams believe. We tend to think that STMs are contributing to significant change because many of the stories we hear are self-reported by teams upon their return.[13] Thus, our assessment of STMs' impact is slanted toward recognizing only the benefits. After two weeks of playing with children, digging wells, and repairing houses, participants return full of stories and examples of how God used them in powerful ways. But these teams are not in the communities two weeks, two months, or two years later. Often the wells break down, the houses slide back into disrepair, and the orphans still do not have stable, long-term relationships in their lives.

Remember: poverty is not just a lack of material resources, and poverty alleviation involves walking with people over time, pointing them to the power of Christ to heal the brokenness in their four key relationships. That process takes time. We should not be surprised that our two-week spurts of building things, handing out clothing, or spending time with children do not have a significant impact in reducing poverty.

A DIFFERENT SORT OF TRIP

As we consider how to engage in short-term trips well, we have to honestly assess our current efforts. A healthy, effective trip is merely one piece of a larger commitment to learning and engagement with what God is doing around the world and in our own communities. Most of this guide will appraise how to practically design and implement trips in ways that support the work of local believers, that promote long-term engagement in missions and poverty alleviation, and that foster lasting change in our own lives.

But first we have to assess the costs of STMs. With potentially three million team members involved in STMs each year and billions of dollars dedicated to these visits, the stakes are too high *not* to ask the hard questions.

TAKEAWAYS

- Consider reading the referenced resources if you wish to more deeply understand the debate concerning the helpfulness of STMs as often practiced.

- Review noted chapters of *When Helping Hurts* to solidify your understanding of poverty and how poverty alleviation fits into God's work.

CHAPTER 2

"DO UNTO OTHERS"

COUNTING THE COSTS
OF STMs

The Golden Rule. Most first graders in your church could recite it by heart, even if they do not fully understand its meaning: "Do unto others as you would have them do unto you." It is part of walking in faithful obedience to our Lord. But sometimes we develop blind spots in our application of the Golden Rule. Certain areas of our vision become obscured by tradition, by incomplete information, or even by good intentions.

Imagine for a moment that your phone rings. It is a friend of a friend calling from Thailand. After a few minutes of small talk, the caller explains that his church in Thailand would like to send twenty-five people, about half of them under the age of eighteen, to your church for two weeks next summer. They understand you are ministering in the low-income apartment complexes around your church, and they want to come help.

The only time they can come is the first two weeks of July, the peak of your church's ministry season. "But don't worry—we are there to help. We've prepped a series of skits, crafts, and lessons to present in VBS classes. We will just hold them in the apartment complex's courtyard," the voice reassures you. "We are bringing gifts for the children to make sure they will attend the VBS, and one of our team members is an electrician who can fix anything in your building while we are there."

A few details must be worked out. The group will have to be picked up from the nearest major airport—a two-hour trip—and they will need places to stay. And they'll expect be fed three meals a day throughout their visit (nothing too out of what they're comfortable with—*what is a casserole, exactly?*) Oh, and one other thing: most of them do not speak English well, if at all. Please arrange translators to accompany them during their stay.

Meanwhile, your church members have spent the past three years gradually developing relationships with the apartment residents and building their trust. The apartment residents are mostly low-income families, and it has taken time for them to feel comfortable with your church's presence in their neighborhood.

While you consider the pros and cons of this offer, the voice continues: "We are just so excited about this opportunity to sacrifice for the sake of the gospel. Our church members are ready and willing to raise $40,000 to come—we are that invested in supporting your work, and depending on how things go, we might explore other opportunities to work together." You know what that last phrase really means: *If we like what we see, we would be willing to give your church ongoing financial support.*

Your church could certainly use the money to purchase new AV equipment and refurbish its nursery. But at what cost? Housing, feeding, and supervising twenty-five people with limited English skills? And what about the relationships at the apartment complex? How will the residents respond to a group of Thais passing out candy and leading VBS sessions?

Do unto others as you would have them do unto you. It sounds so simple. Until it isn't.

BUCKLE YOUR SEAT BELTS

Before you jump into this chapter, be forewarned: if you are looking for light bedtime reading to make you feel happy about the current state of Western missions and poverty alleviation, you will probably want to save this chapter for tomorrow. As described in the introduction, this guide is designed as a practical resource that casts a vision for what short-term trips can be when used as part of a long-term process of engagement. However, the vision cast and the guidelines we suggest in the coming chapters were not developed in a vacuum. They are designed to counter and prevent the very real harm that many STMs are causing. Further, crucial stewardship questions must be humbly considered as we move forward in retooling STMs.

Not every concern in this chapter applies to every short-term trip. Thankfully, many churches and organizations are intentionally working to prevent harm through their trips. But it is easy to nod enthusiastically as you read through this chapter, thinking, "We don't do any of these things—but I hope other churches or ministries are listening." Please read this chapter with an open mind and soft heart. Honestly consider where you might need to change.

It's time to look in the proverbial mirror and see how—and why— STMs need a reformation.

DOLLARS AND CENTS

When tallying the cost of STMs, we have to begin with the math: just how much money do STMs cost, and are they a responsible use of the resources God has entrusted to us?

The financial cost of STMs is difficult to pin down, given the variety of locations and types of trips. In 2008 research, Robert J. Priest, professor of mission and anthropology at Trinity Evangelical Divinity School, and Joseph Paul Priest, a sociologist and missions expert, estimate that the average cost of an international STM is around $1400 per person.[1] Based on a 2005 survey, Robert Wuthnow and Stephen Offutt estimate that 1.6 million US adults travel on an international STM each year.[2] In light of these two pieces of research, the cost of *only* adult, international STMs could easily add up to over *$2.2 billion* per year. As Wuthnow points out, even a conservative figure of $1.6 billion would pay *the yearly wages* of roughly four million people living in extreme poverty.[3]

The fact that so much money is being spent is *not* the problem. As comparably affluent believers, we should be giving even more to ministry and to poverty alleviation efforts in our own communities and around the world. We need to be more generous, not less. What is troubling is how inefficiently that money is used when allocated to traditional STMs.

Economists talk about something called *opportunity cost*. For every investment of our resources, whether time, money, or energy, there is something else we could have done with those resources instead. When a student chooses to watch a movie the night before a test, the opportunity cost of that action is the higher grade they could have obtained through studying. When we spend all day shopping to find the cheapest pair of shoes, the opportunity cost is the time and gas money we sacrifice to find the better deal.

Opportunity cost is ultimately about stewardship. Are we, as affluent believers and churches, choosing to allocate the resources God has given us in the most responsible way, or are we ignoring the other things we could have done with those gifts? Jo Ann Van Engen, who has served on the mission field in Honduras for years, shares a sobering story:

> A group of eighteen students raised $25,000 to fly to Honduras for spring break. They painted an orphanage, cleaned the playground, and played with the children. . . . The Honduran orphanage's yearly budget is $45,000. That covers the staff's salaries, building maintenance, and food and clothes for the children. One staff member there confided, "The amount that group raised for their week here is more than half our working budget. We could have done so much with that money."[4]

Kurt Ver Beek studied the effectiveness of STM trips to Honduras following Hurricane Mitch and discovered similar trends. Building a house in Honduras using local workers and resources (i.e., without

STM teams) cost roughly $2,000. Each STM construction team typically built one house—but they spent $30,000 on the trip.[5] The money each team spent could have built *fifteen* homes if it had been entrusted to local organizations and built using local labor and resources.

Or consider the typical salary of local Christians ministering in the Majority World. Gospel for Asia, an organization that supports local believers as they plant churches in their own countries, reports that average monthly support for local missionaries ranges from $120–$360.[6] At the *high end* of that spectrum, a yearly salary would be $4,320. The money spent on a $30,000 STM could support almost seven local church planters for a year. Likewise, Majority World Christian relief and development workers at the community level commonly earn annual salaries ranging from $3,000–$6,000. A $30,000 STM could support five to ten workers. That is quite the opportunity cost.

But there is another element to the opportunity cost of STMs. Hosting STMs requires incredible amounts of work and coordination from the receiving community and host. Dennis Horton, a professor at Baylor University, surveyed one hundred long-term workers who hosted STMs, investigating their perspective on the positive and negative elements of short-term trips. Almost 40 percent of the respondents listed the time and energy consumed by STMs as a negative impact. For example, a missionary couple in Southeast Asia described it this way: "When an STM team is on the ground, there's really no down time for the host. You feel 24/7 'on' until the team departs because you are responsible for their housing, food, safety, health, transportation, 'good experience,' most everything. Add prep time and recovery time afterward, and a one-week STM likely consumes four weeks of true work time."[7]

Missions agencies and organizations also invest significant human resources in STM programs. Scott Moreau, professor of intercultural studies at Wheaton College, researched staffing trends in missions agencies from 1996 to 2005. He discovered that from 1996 to 2005, the number of staff members dedicating some portion of their time to STMs increased by almost 218 percent. Within that growth, the number of workers dedicating *all* of their time to STMs grew by almost 325 percent.[8] Considering the financial resources needed to support those positions, as well as what else these workers could do with their time, the opportunity cost is astounding.

Then why, despite their high costs and relatively small positive impacts, do STMs continue to grow? On one level, some local churches and organizations are uncomfortable saying no to STM teams due to cultural and socioeconomic realities. But on another level, STMs serve as a funding mechanism for some organizations. When a team raises money for an STM through an intermediary organization, missions agency, or even a local ministry, part of those funds *may* go to support its operating and long-term program expenses. In these scenarios, rocking the proverbial STM boat threatens funding for long-term work, making some ministries and workers very hesitant to push back.

But here is the question: why can't we, as believers blessed with incredible financial resources, freely give our money to effective workers and organizations without spending additional thousands upon thousands of dollars on a trip every year? Yes, part of the cost of a trip may support long-term work. But it is the epitome of an inefficient funding source.

What does it say about us, as the Western church, that we often are unwilling to support work without seeing it ourselves? When describing the benefits of STMs, James Lai, a missions leader in Asia, argues that STMs "satisfy and mobilize the postmodernists. The postmodernist congregation does not like just to be told about missions but to be hands-on themselves."[9] That could be seen as a benefit of STMs. But should it have to be this way? Could it be that the popularity of STMs is partially an outgrowth of our insatiable need for emotional experiences to validate faith and obedience?

As a counterargument, some people would argue that the money spent on STMs would not be given to long-term work anyway, so stewardship concerns are null and void. But again: what does that say about us? It's time to die to self, setting aside our desires and considering what can best edify the kingdom (see Ephesians 4:20–24). It's time to "value others above" ourselves (Philippians 2:3), scrutinizing even our good intentions for traces of self-centeredness. Obviously good steward-ship requires accountability, and congregations are right to ensure that their support is being used responsibly. But that does not require send-ing forty people to a different location twice a year. We should con-sider trimming our spending and scale of trips, and instead give that money to proven, trusted organizations that are engaged in effective, asset-based development work via local churches and workers. Shifting giving toward long-term work is dramatically countercultural within many Christian circles: sacrificing for the sake of the Great Commis-sion may mean *not* going on an STM. It may mean *not* touching the work. Instead, it may mean all of us should give dramatically more to reputable organizations, ministries, and workers, people whom God has already placed within communities to engage in long-term, effec-tive ministry.

At first glance, it may seem that scaling back on STMs and scal-ing up our giving undermines the relational nature of missions. But nothing could be further from the truth. Writing a check can free our brothers and sisters around the world to engage in long-term, highly relational work in their own communities. These brothers and sisters know the local language and culture, and they have preexisting con-nections in these communities that we simply do not have. Through our generosity, we can foster ministry that is far more relational than anything we could ever do through a two-week trip.

We have to count the cost. Short-term trips can be done well, and this guide is designed to move churches and ministries forward in that process. The key to making trips worth the investment is situating the trip as merely one piece in a longer learning experience, moving par-ticipants forward in long-term engagement with missions and effective poverty alleviation. But the current cost and outcomes are not defen-sible from a stewardship perspective.

DO NO HARM

Today's STM model does not just raise questions of opportunity cost. We also have to consider the potential damage done to low-income communities through STMs, as they often violate several key principles of poverty alleviation. (See chapter 7 of *When Helping Hurts* for a longer discussion.)

Inappropriately Providing Relief

Much of the damage caused by STMs stems from the fact that they tend to apply "relief" when "development" is the form of poverty alleviation that the context actually requires. Relief is the temporary and free provision of material goods following a man-made crisis or natural disaster. But when people are in a chronic state of poverty, development is the appropriate intervention. While relief is done *for* people, development walks *with* people, encouraging them to use their gifts and resources to contribute to their own progress. Among other things, development includes empowering the materially poor to glorify God through work and to support themselves and their families with the fruit of that work. (See chapter 4 of *When Helping Hurts* for a further elaboration of the differences between relief and development.)

Most STMs to low-income communities are working in contexts that require development, not relief. Unfortunately, because many STM teams think that poverty is fundamentally about a lack of material resources rather than broken relationships, the teams often default to relief work by giving handouts of material resources: shoes, clothes, food, houses, money, etc. When team after team engages in such practices, they create a crippling system of paternalism: habitually doing things or providing things for people that they are able to provide or do for themselves.[10] This fosters dependency in the community, undermining long-term progress.

In addition, STMs that provide relief inappropriately can undermine the local economy. How can a local seamstress compete with free clothing being handed out by a different STM team each month? Furthermore, STMs often do work that local people could be employed to do. The money spent sending an STM to paint a building could be used to pay local people, providing them with work and income to support their families.[11] A Haitian missionary surveyed in Dennis Horton's research put it this way: "I don't agree with having groups do work that could easily create jobs in a country with 80% unemployment."[12]

Finally, the provider-receiver dynamic inherent to relief work, if applied outside the context of a crisis, can deepen poor communities' existing feelings of inferiority or inadequacy. Part of the way the materially poor are broken—a sense of shame and powerlessness—and part of the way that we are broken—a sense of pride and "god-complexes"—do not mix well. (See chapter 2 of *When Helping Hurts*.) The ways that we speak and act toward the materially poor tend to confirm in them what they are often already feeling: "I am inferior; I can't do it; I need somebody to help change my situation." This attitude can make them more passive, and, as this happens, we often become more arrogant. Though typically on a subconscious level, we begin to think, "They must not have the capabilities and initiative to change their situation. I am so glad I came to help them." Their sense of inadequacy is deepened, and our pride is enhanced.

David Livermore, who has spent years studying cross-cultural engagement and short-term missions, shares a story that illustrates this dynamic. He and his wife, Linda, and their daughters were visiting Malaysia. After seeing a materially poor Malay father and daughter on the street, Livermore encouraged his own daughter to give the little girl a frog stuffed animal.

> As we started to leave, the Malay father ordered his daughter to return the frog. We motioned that we didn't want it back, but he insisted. He began to raise his voice and grabbed the frog and handed it to me. . . . As I began to talk with Linda about it, we thought back to our home in the Chicago area. Though a beautiful house, our home was one of the more modest homes in our town. Linda asked, "So how would you feel if one of the parents in the million-dollar homes near us suddenly walked up to our girls and started handing them gifts?" All of a sudden I began to see this in a new light. I thought about how I would feel if some rich person started giving my girls unsolicited gifts in my presence. I'm quite capable of caring for them, thank you![13]

Livermore did not anticipate that giving a stuffed animal—something he intended as an act of generosity—would provoke such a negative response. Livermore's intentions were good, but he angered and shamed the Malay father by implying that he could not adequately provide for his own child.

Focusing on Needs Rather Than Assets

STMs also tend to focus on needs of a community rather than its assets. A needs-based approach to poverty alleviation focuses on the perceived deficits or shortcomings in a materially poor community and positions the outsiders as the primary source of improvement. This approach tends to exacerbate the god-complexes of STM participants and the sense of inferiority on the part of materially poor people.

In contrast, asset-based development seeks to acknowledge, celebrate, and mobilize the existing spiritual, human, material, and social resources in a low-income community. The goal is to help the materially poor to discover their own resources and abilities and to start stewarding those gifts more effectively. Outside resources are then used to appropriately build on the community's resources. In addition to building local sustainability, an asset-based approach can help to overcome the god-complexes of the outsiders and the feelings of inferiority on the part of many poor people.

Unfortunately, most STMs take a needs-based approach, loading human and material resources into vans and airplanes, never stopping to ask what abilities and resources may already be present in the communities they are seeking to serve. (See chapter 5 of *When Helping Hurts* for a further discussion of needs-based and asset-based approaches.)

Using Blueprint Rather Than Participatory Approaches

The blueprint approach to poverty alleviation consists of outsiders determining what poor communities need and then imposing those predetermined solutions on them. This approach tends to deepen the god-complexes of the outsiders and to deepen the sense of inferiority of the poor, as the former treats the latter as objects.

In contrast, participatory approaches treat poor people as what they are: image-bearers called to steward their own gifts and resources. Participatory development asks poor individuals and communities what they think should be done and how it should be done, walking alongside them in a process of mutual learning and discovery. By giving priority to the voices and goals of the poor, participatory approaches can again help to overcome the god-complex-inferiority dynamic.

Unfortunately, most STMs tend toward blueprint rather than participatory development. Team leaders plan what they want to do *to* poor communities—without much, if any, input from those communities about what should be done or even if the team is wanted at all. (See chapter 6 of *When Helping Hurts* for further elaboration of blueprint and participatory development.)

In summary, STMs often undermine asset-based, participatory development that is at the very heart of effective poverty alleviation. In many instances, this does real harm to the same poor people these STMs are seeking to help, by creating crippling dependencies, by intensifying already-existing feelings of shame, and by undermining the stewardship of local resources. In addition, such STMs often fuel the pride and god-complexes of those who go.

Do not overlook the colossal tragedy in all of this. The church of Jesus Christ is spending billions of dollars annually on approaches that often do lasting harm both to materially poor people and to those of us who are seeking to serve them. The poor deserve better than this . . . our King deserves better than this.

SUPPORTING OR UNDERMINING?

Beyond directly harming the materially poor, STMs often inadvertently undercut the work of local development workers and churches. James Ward, director of international programs at the 410 Bridge, an organization encouraging long-term, community-initiated development in rural Majority World communities, shares an unfortunate scenario:

We have very clear policies regarding handouts on trips: because of the danger of dependency and unhealthy giving, participants are never to give something away—not a bottle of water, not a leftover bag of chips, not a pair of shoes. We do not want to build relationships with the community based on what we give, but rather on how we can use our strengths to serve each other. One time, one of our communities was working on a primary school and invited a short-term team to participate. To make a long story short, the team members disregarded our guidelines and gave clothes, shoes, and other handouts to the children. . . . The next time the local staff tried to return to the school and continue our engagement with them, the children, and even the staff, expected more handouts. The terms of the relationship had totally changed. They now expected money and handouts from our organization. We could no longer send teams to the school, and the damage from that one team took literally years to repair.[14]

In a similar way, STMs can also set an unattainable standard of what "church" is supposed to be. Consider the following observation of an American staff member who works with a local development organization in a Latin American country:

The indigenous staff in my organization lead weekly Bible studies with children in low-income communities. These Bible studies are just one aspect of my organization's overall attempts to bring long-lasting development in these broken communities. After a short-term team conducts a Bible study in one of these communities, the children stop attending the Bible studies of my organization. Our indigenous staff tell me that the children stop coming because we do not have all the fancy materials and crafts that the short-term teams have, and we do not give away things like these teams do. The children have also come to believe that our staff are not as interesting or as creative as the Americans that come on these teams.[15]

No STM team would ever intend to hurt the work of local churches. But we often do not stop to think—or more importantly to ask our brothers and sisters in receiving communities—about the long-term consequences of our actions. Many churches or organizations rarely share these concerns, deciding to accommodate STMs anyway because of the foundational social, cultural, or financial power dynamics of the STM relationship. This includes churches or organizations that choose not to push back because a portion of their funding is tied to their supporting churches bringing teams to their community.

The point of sharing these stories is not to judge people's intentions or hearts. Instead, the goal is to illustrate that the fundamental assumptions, goals, structure, and methods of STMs as they exist today are setting us up to unintentionally harm materially poor communities and the ministries that work in them.

SELF-DESTRUCTIVE TENDENCIES

Reforming the way we do STMs is not just a matter of preventing harm in materially poor communities. STMs also have a tendency to exacerbate our own brokenness, our god-complexes and misconceptions about the materially poor. STMs often focus on the needs of a community. We see all the things they "lack," and we see ourselves as the ones who can meet those needs. What often develops is a subconscious messiah-complex, an attitude in which we see ourselves as having to save materially poor communities. We forget that God created them with gifts and abilities that they can use to steward their resources and improve their own lives. When we treat low-income communities like they are helpless, we inflate our own sense of importance. And we fail to see our own need for a Savior.

David Livermore highlights this dynamic, recounting an unsettling conversation with Majority World pastors:

> "[Team members] talk about us to your churches back home in such demeaning ways." I pushed back. "Really? You guys come off as heroes in the reports I hear. You would think your churches were near perfect from what most short-termers say about you." They weren't so sure. Our exaggerations about how nationals are so dependent upon these short-term teams, the long-term impact suggested by the work, the jokes about the weird foods given and the destitute conditions, and

the exaggerated reports about what was accomplished often lead our brothers and sisters to feel demeaned.[16]

These types of conversations should make us seriously examine our own attitudes as we engage in STMs. STMs should lead us to respect the poor as image-bearers and brothers and sisters in Christ even more, not view ourselves as their rescuers. We are both utterly dependent on the healing work of Christ in our lives, without whom we are *all* helpless.

There is another subtle danger in STMs: it is easy for us to feel like we have successfully met our biblical mandate to love and care for the poor because we participated in an STM. As we saw in chapter 1, even though many STM participants return with stories of how their lives have been changed by seeing and meeting the needs of the materially poor, comparatively few of those people become more involved in supporting the ministry they visited or in ministering in their own communities. There is simply not much consistent, long-term increase in most participants' financial support, advocacy, or volunteer work when they return.

Unfortunately, engaging in messy, long-term relationships with the materially poor next door is more difficult than playing with children for two weeks in Kenya or reroofing houses in rural Appalachia. Think about the crisis pregnancy centers or after-school tutoring programs in our own areas. How can service with these institutions possibly look as attractive as many STMs, with the allure of travel, scenery, and the feeling of quick and easy accomplishment?

As church and ministry leaders, we must never elevate participation in an STM as an indicator of spiritual maturity or passion for missions. It may reflect such maturity and passion, but it should be accompanied by lasting engagement. And we certainly should not judge those who have never participated in a trip.

It is time to stop, listen, and reflect on how short-term trips are commonly practiced in our own churches. Remember: trips need to be reformed, not destroyed. They have incredible potential to be a part of blessing both participants and receiving communities. But moving forward with a healthier structure and approach to STMs requires humility. It requires us to step back and ask, "Are we really doing unto others as we would have them do unto us if we were living in their context?"

Answering that question requires listening and learning from those brothers and sisters. And as we will see, short-term trips can play a powerful role in that process, deepening our understanding of and engagement with what God is doing in the world.

TAKEAWAYS

- While the stewardship questions surrounding STMs still leave space for healthy visits, seriously consider what the opportunity cost means for the purpose of a trip.

- Review the noted chapters of *When Helping Hurts* to solidify your understanding of why STMs cannot directly engage in poverty alleviation—and how they might actually undermine poverty alleviation.

- Be sure you and the team understand and are committed to avoiding relief work (i.e., the provider-receiver dynamic) on the field. This is one of the biggest battles you may face with team members.

CHAPTER 3

PRESENCE OR PROJECTS

A PATH FORWARD

We know the past two chapters were rather heavy. But we have good news. There is a place for short-term trips in the body of Christ. But they must be built on a fundamentally different framework than most trips currently are. David Livermore recounts a story about a short-term team his church sent to Rwanda that illustrates a way forward:

> Within their first hour in Rwanda, the local team said, "Ninety percent of your job is done. You're here, your presence speaks volumes." One of the team members told me she thought, "Well, I don't think so. That's gracious of you, but we're here to work hard." The longer she was there, however, the more she began to see that the tasks they came to do were not what was needed most. The presence and chance for relationship together seemed to be the most pressing need for the Rwandan church beyond any menial tasks that were planned.[1]

"Your presence speaks volumes." What would it look like if we considered a healthy presence—rather than our knowledge, resources, or ideas—the most important to bring when arriving on the field?

CASTING A DIFFERENT VISION

When properly designed, short-term trips are *an opportunity to learn from, encourage, and fellowship with believers around the world in the context of long-term engagement with God's work, focusing on understanding His body and our role in it more fully.* This chapter will look at the basic elements of this retooled model. Just as a reminder, this material is tailored to address trips of laypeople from your congregation; chapter 5 will address particular elements of trips designed for strategic partnership development.

The current STM approach is firmly entrenched in our church subculture. A helpful initial step can be changing the vocabulary that we use to describe trips, distinguishing between existing practices and where we want to be. The current term, "short-term mission trip," contains a two-fold problem. First, "mission" brings to mind going and doing direct ministry *to* and *for* the materially poor. Second, emphasizing "trip" focuses on the time spent in another place. Consider creating a term that emphasizes *learning* rather than *doing.*

Avoid the word "trip" in formal titles, and use language that captures the eight- to twelve-month commitment you are asking of participants. Consider using titles and descriptions like "Learn-Encourage-Engage" or "Learn and Respond Journeys." Be creative, and find something that works for your congregation and context. Within this guide, we will use the words "visit" or "trip" when specifically referencing time spent on the field, but always within the context of the trip or visit being one piece of the learning and long-term engagement process. We will continue to use the phrase "short-term mission (STM)" to describe trips as currently and commonly practiced.

One last warning before we begin: it is tempting to use new language to label STMs without actually changing their substance or structure. If the only thing you change after reading this book is the title of your STMs, *then you have not actually accomplished anything.* As Sam Moore, a community development specialist, shared, "There is an enormous danger of the mainstream church using the language of 'best-practices' to feel better about its efforts, but then never actually implementing best-practices. I am afraid all that is happening is that churches are making a new set of vocabulary into meaningless jargon."[2]

LEARNING FROM THE "WEAK" AND "LOWLY"

One of the primary purposes of a visit is to fellowship as equals with the believers we encounter, leading to long-term engagement with missions and poverty alleviation as we listen to and learn from these believers. Consider Paul's command to the Corinthian church in 1 Corinthians 1:26–31:

> Brothers and sisters, think of what you were when you were called. Not many of you were wise by human standards; not many were influential; not many were of noble birth. But God chose the foolish things of the world to shame the wise; God chose the weak things of the world to shame the strong. God chose the lowly things of this world and the despised things—and the things that are not—to nullify the things that are, so that no one may boast before him. It is because of him that you are in Christ Jesus, who has become for us wisdom from God—that is, our righteousness, holiness and redemption. Therefore, as it is written: "Let the one who boasts boast in the Lord."

God does not call His children because they are exceptional. He does not choose the perfect, the wealthy, or the influential. Healthy trips are rooted in the refrain of praise: "Let us boast in the Lord together! Let us celebrate the things He has done in our lives through Christ." *No one has grounds to boast in their own accomplishments.* Ultimately, 1 Corinthians 1 describes an attitude of humility and mutual encouragement, not an attitude focused on fixing those the world calls "weak."

As brothers and sisters in Christ, we are called to listen to each other, valuing and learning from the wisdom and experiences that God has given to each of us. Believers in the slums of Kenya understand God's provision and sustaining presence in ways that many more affluent Christians do not. African-American brothers and sisters in Birmingham, Alabama, have much to teach Caucasian believers about suffering and forgiveness. But if short-term trips are built around "doing," accomplishing particular tasks and projects, they cannot create the time or safe space necessary for this type of listening and learning.

It is one thing to say that God uses the "weak things of the world to shame the strong." But when we, as relatively affluent Christians, step into a materially poor community, it is easy to be overwhelmed by the needs around us. *There are homeless people living under every overpass. There is no running water. They don't have desks in their schools—scratch that, they don't even have school buildings.* The needs within a community appear like flashing red lights around us, and it is tempting to slip back into an attitude of "doing" and "fixing." Focusing primarily on their needs, however real they may be, initiates the very dynamic that poisons our relationships: a dynamic that says we are superior, they are inferior, and we are the only ones with the power to change their situation.

Maintaining a 1 Corinthians 1 attitude toward our brothers and sisters requires that we proactively look for and respect the assets God has graciously placed in every community, instead of focusing on needs. As we see their gifts and abilities, we start to view them as God does, helping us overcome our sense of superiority, our own poverty of being, and laying the basis for effective learning.

Going as learners also means we seek to understand the context of our brothers' and sisters' lives. If we believe that Christ is the creator, sustainer, and reconciler of all things, not just our souls, then learning about His work and His people means learning about their political, environmental, social, cultural, and religious context. Part of a visit to inner-city Memphis should include better understanding how God used the church in this city during the Civil Rights movement. In a different vein, a team in Haiti should understand the origins and impact of voodoo on Haitian culture, and how the local church is responding to this challenge.

Michael and Shelley, missionaries who hosted short-term teams for seventeen years in a Majority World country, describe what this learning process looked like in their ministry:

> We did what we called "conversational dinners." Our groups would sit on an open-air porch around a single table for dinner, and various members of the community would join us four or five times throughout the week. The guests were very different—farmers, pastors, students, or housewives. One at a time, they would eat with us and we

would all swap stories and small talk. After supper, they would share about their worlds. The teacher would talk about the educational challenges in the community. The pastor would talk about spiritual warfare. The student would explain his or her typical day, how he or she would walk three to four miles to school or do homework by candlelight. The visiting teams learned so much about the culture and lives of their brothers and sisters.[3]

Beyond the spiritual and educational significance of these interactions, research has shown that directly interacting with local community members and church leaders contributes to reducing team members' paternalistic tendencies.[4] It is more difficult to take a posture of superiority after experiencing these types of direct learning encounters, which can foster a 1 Corinthians 1 attitude in our hearts. It also places the materially poor in a position of "teacher," which can combat any sense of inferiority they experience.

BREAKING BREAD TOGETHER

Learning and cross-cultural engagement is a positive outcome from visits, but going as learners does not mean that we are unable to bless or serve the people we encounter. Rather, it opens up new, deeply enriching ways for us to love our brothers and sisters in Christ, namely through fellowshiping with and encouraging them.

The kingdom of God and the body of Christ are global, cross-cultural entities. When we fellowship and worship together, we are proclaiming to the rest of the world whose we are, and saying to each other, "I am in this with you. We serve the same God. We are saved by the same sacrifice. You are not alone."

Focusing on fellowship and being together, as opposed to particular projects, also fosters an attitude of respect and mutuality in which our hosts can use *their* gifts. Marco Perez, who led a Bible school in Latin America for eleven years, describes his vision for receiving short-term teams this way: "We hosted many short-term teams during my time at the Bible school. Before the teams came, I always told the staff at my school, 'Look, there is a youth group coming in for the week. Chances are, they are planning on fixing things. In reality, this is an opportunity to minister to them. That's our goal, and that's how I want you to interact with them.'"[5]

The early church has much to teach us about engaging in this type of fellowship and encouragement. Yes, the current scale of short-term trips is only possible because of the technological advancements of the past sixty years. But we make a huge mistake if we think that the Bible does not have anything to say about how we should interact with believers from a different context.

When you read the book of Acts and Paul's letters, it is amazing how many church leaders were crisscrossing the Roman world. Paul. Silas. Barnabas. Apollos. Timothy. And they often took other believers with them from one congregation to another (see passages such as Acts 15:22–35 and Acts 18:18–28). In addition, the congregations and church leaders invested in each other over time, esteeming and exhorting one another as members of the body of Christ. These churches were from different cultural and religious backgrounds, lived under varying levels of persecution, and represented a range of economic classes. They did not have video chat, email, or air travel. And yet they were deeply engaged with one another. They prayed for each other, they sent greetings to each other, they longed to hear about each other's work and life. And above all, they encouraged one another.

Paul, writing to the Romans while in prison, says that he longs to see them again, "that you and I may be mutually encouraged by each other's faith" (Romans 1:12). This is Paul, an apostle and author of fourteen books of the New Testament, craving the encouragement of and fellowship with the Roman believers. In the conclusion of Ephesians, Paul says that he sent Tychicus, "the dear brother and faithful servant in the Lord," to the Ephesians "that you may know how we are, and that he may encourage you" (Ephesians 6:21–22).

Consider this story from a ministry leader who now realizes the value of encouragement:

> I was leading a team of youth on a short-term trip to a very secular
> part of Europe. We had anticipated the primary focus being projects

on the church building, or outreach to the low-income community around the church. Instead, when we got there, the pastor greeted the team and said, "All I care about is that you have breakfast, lunch, and dinner with members of our church every day. This isn't the easiest place to be a Christian—there aren't tons of passionate believers around us. I want your presence and passion to be refreshing to our church." At first, I found the notion strange. Eating meals with church members? But then I realized, "What a beautiful example of what a short-term trip can be."[6]

Paul, in Colossians 4:7–16, closes his letter with an incredible picture of this type of engagement and relationship in the body of Christ:

Tychicus will tell you all the news about me. He is a dear brother, a faithful minister and fellow servant in the Lord. I am sending him to you for the express purpose that you may know about our circumstances and that he may encourage your hearts. He is coming with Onesimus, our faithful and dear brother, who is one of you. They will tell you everything that is happening here.

My fellow prisoner Aristarchus sends you his greetings, as does Mark, the cousin of Barnabas. (You have received instructions about him; if he comes to you, welcome him.) Jesus, who is called Justus, also sends greetings. These are the only Jews among my coworkers for the kingdom of God, and they have proved a comfort to me. Epaphras, who is one of you and a servant of Christ Jesus, sends greetings. He is always wrestling in prayer for you, that you may stand firm in all the will of God, mature and fully assured. I vouch for him that he is working hard for you and for those at Laodicea and Hierapolis. Our dear friend Luke, the doctor, and Demas send greetings. Give my greetings to the brothers and sisters at Laodicea, and to Nympha and the church in her house.

After this letter has been read to you, see that it is also read in the church of the Laodiceans and that you in turn read the letter from Laodicea.

It seems like the "meat" of Paul's message is complete before these personal remarks at the end of the book. But it is not. Not every church will have a direct relationship with a congregation miles away; some will support local workers and believers via third-party organizations. But regardless, we are all called to have an attitude of love, humility, and respect like the one Paul describes toward receiving communities.

SEEING THE DIGNITY, NOT IGNORING THE PAIN

Going as learners and encouragers focused on the gifts God has put in low-income communities does not mean we dismiss the harsh reality of material poverty—or the acute forms of pain that accompany it. The goal is not to simply see poverty as irrelevant, or to view material poverty itself as a spiritual virtue or as a mark of more authentic faith. Rather, the goal is to affirm the dignity of the materially poor in the midst of their very real pain, and learn from them as they experience things that many affluent Christians have never faced.

The following is a story from Jason, who has led trips as part of long-term engagement with orphans, many of whom are now young adults:

> I never understood the place of lament in our faith [before]. One night during a praise service, several of the youth just broke down crying, and then doubled over screaming. They began sobbing, "Why, why, why," and "It hurts, it hurts, it hurts," and "Why did they leave me?" It was gut-wrenching. We didn't know how to process that. It sent us, as a team and congregation, on years of exploring what worship looks like out of a context of pain and distress. None of that was in the gospel that we consciously brought with us to that community. But it is a part of the gospel that the Spirit led us to through our relationships with them. We read our Bibles, especially the Psalms, in new ways. . . . Because of these types of encounters, some participants have even pursued formal training in trauma therapy and counseling. They are now using that training in our own community and as we continue to walk alongside our brothers and sisters overseas.[7]

The key is that Jason and his team did not try to "fix" the youth or respond with patronizing pity. They humbly entered into their world as learners, and then shared their burdens.

WORKING TOGETHER

In the context of respectful partnerships where we view ourselves as learners and encouragers, there may be an opportunity to enter into particular projects or tasks *alongside* our brothers and sisters. But projects should not be the focus of a visit, and we should never take a leadership role. Local community members must be the ones initiating, organizing, and executing any tasks. Therefore, recognize that timing is everything. Planning for a trip starts months in advance, and there is no guarantee that the community will be ready to incorporate project assistance in a healthy way when a team actually arrives. Teams must always be willing *not* to engage in a project if doing so would undermine the leadership and participation of the community.

Kurt Kandler, executive director of the 410 Bridge, an organization that sends short-term teams to support community-initiated, sustainable development work, describes healthy project involvement this way:

> If a community has identified and started work on a project, like digging a well or expanding a road, they will invite a team to join them. But if local community members don't show up to lead and work when it is time to pull out the shovels, our indigenous staff will literally put the team back on the bus. We will not do the work without the community—doing so would undermine the long-term process of the community owning its own change. But most of the time, the community turns out in droves. It's like a "honey-do" list. If I have a list of projects I need to do around the house and my brother-in-law or father are coming to join me, I'll be ready. It is always more fun and encouraging doing it together—it's actually about the relationship, not the project. We talk while we work, we catch up about our lives, and we accomplish the tasks while engaging with each other. But I could do it on my own, and I would never expect him to just come do it *for* me while I watch. Our local staff approaches the development work with short-term teams in a similar way.[8]

This attitude of seeing any "work" the team does as only complementing the work of community members is crucial. Remember: development is "doing with," not "doing for."

WORKING IN RELIEF CONTEXTS

Short-term teams do occasionally enter situations calling for relief, meaning that doing tasks for people in crisis or distributing material goods may be needed. However, this is extremely rare. By the time most teams arrive at the field following a disaster, the initial "bleeding" has stopped and the context requires "rehabilitation," not relief. Rehabilitation entails working with people as they return to pre-crisis conditions, as opposed to simply giving them things. If you are methodically moving through this guide before your trip, the chances of relief being the required intervention on a community level are extremely low. However, if your church quickly mobilizes a team for a relief context in the future, here are a few things to keep in mind:

- Go where you have a partner organization that has requested additional manpower or specialized abilities, and that has the infrastructure to host and deploy your team. Simply showing up on the scene of a crisis can often create more chaos: Where will you stay? What about transportation? How will you integrate your team with the work already happening?

- Do not go if you do not know the language. Well-meaning teams often arrive at an area and divert the energy and time of local workers and translators already engaged in effective relief. While exceptions to this rule sometimes exist for people with specialized skills, such as a team of surgeons or search and rescue professionals, you will still need a group to help you plug in effectively.

- Avoid bringing resources with you unless specifically requested by your local contacts. In some scenarios, such as after a huge earthquake, there may be widespread shortages of particular goods. However, in cases like tornados or tsunamis, the disaster-struck area can be comparatively small, surrounded by totally unaffected areas. There may be ample resources and intact infrastructure a mere few miles away. Mobilizing those resources, if available, is more efficient and is better for the local economy.

• Only go if you are physically, emotionally, and mentally suited for the work. In a true relief context, physical strength and stamina are often essential, whether for clearing debris or working incredibly long hours. Seeing the devastation of a catastrophe is also emotionally taxing. Take people who will be able to process and function through seeing very difficult things.

DESIGNED DIFFERENTLY[9]

On a practical level, what does it look like when a trip is designed according to the framework described in this chapter? Here are a few initial applications. Be sure that any intermediary organization you are going with is operating on these principles, or build your trip around them as you work directly with a local organization or ministry:

• **Engage for the Long Haul:** Since trips are not about self-contained accomplishments and doing, deliberately lead participants in pre- and post-trip learning, making the trip merely one stage in a journey of connecting more deeply with God's work in the world and in your community. Otherwise, you risk poorly stewarding the resources invested in the trip. Thanks to the Internet, you may also have opportunities to engage in ongoing conversation and prayer with your partners. Visits are far more encouraging for both parties if you continue to support the work your brothers and sisters are doing, rather than consuming a short-term trip as an exciting experience. In some cases, that process of long-term engagement may only warrant or require one full trip, providing enough context and understanding to support your brothers and sisters as they work in their own communities. In other cases, the trip may be one piece of an ongoing partnership as your church explores future opportunities.

- **Submit to Local Leadership:** Visits must be rooted in humility and respect for local workers, believers, and organizations. This reality should shape everything about trips, beginning with whether or not they even occur. A truly healthy trip can only happen when local believers, workers, or organizations initiate it. Further, it is difficult to learn from and appropriately value your brothers and sisters if you are dictating the terms of the relationship, making decisions about the content, schedule, and size of the trip without their initiation, buy-in, and participation.

- **Keep Teams Small:** While the ideal team size varies based on the specific context of your trip, trips of more than ten to fifteen people make maintaining a learning and fellowship emphasis extremely difficult. Some research has shown that many hosts prefer even smaller groups ranging from five to nine people.[10] Ultimately, it is important to adhere to whatever size limit your host requests.

- **Require Participant Financial Investment:** In the same way that low-income communities and individuals are more likely to "own" improvement if they financially contribute to the change process, participants are more likely to take the trip seriously if they sacrifice their own hard-earned cash toward the trip. The amount of personal financial contribution will vary based on the type of trip, the age of the participants, and your congregation's context, but the amount should be neither so small that it is token or so large that it prevents participation. There will be times when some team members, due to their financial situation, will need to contribute less than others. But requiring some form of personal investment is essential to designing a trip focused on long-term engagement.

- **Study the Context:** Spend time researching the political, economic, cultural, and spiritual context of the location you will be visiting and be prepared to lead your team through this learning. How does the history of the local church differ from the history of the church in your area? How does their culture differ from your own? What systemic factors, such as political unrest, economic exploitation, and religious oppression, have contributed to poverty? Working through these types of questions before even recruiting your team members will equip you to cast a vision focused on learning and valuing the unique gifts within the community. As a result, your team will be better prepared to soak in and process the things they see during the visit, rather than just letting them pass by in the midst of excitement, confusion, and exhaustion. As Brian Howell, professor of anthropology at Wheaton College, argues, the more you can communicate that learning is a legitimate and essential component of the trip, not an add-on, the better.[11]

- **Prioritize Time for Learning, Fellowship, and Encouragement:** Live life alongside your brothers and sisters while on your trip, learning from their experiences, worshiping with them, and spending time with local community leaders. In the planning process, humbly ask your hosts whether there might be local people willing to be a part of intentional times of learning and exchange like Michael and Shelley's "conversational dinners." As always, be humble in this process and trust your local hosts' judgment about whether, how, and when these interactions should occur given cultural differences and contextual factors. The last thing you want to create is a dynamic in which local people feel like they have been put on display for the sake of educating outsiders.

So let's explore what offering our *presence*, simply being with and learning from our brothers and sisters, might look like. Doing so will bless and love them in deeper ways than offering temporary material goods could. In the process, we can support them in their work, leading to lasting change and poverty alleviation over time.

TAKEAWAYS

- Create a name for visits that captures the broader learning and engagement process; find a title that will work for your particular church context. Remember: do not merely focus on taking a trip.

- Reflecting on the Designed Differently points above, what do you think these elements might look like in your particular church and context?

PART TWO

· · ·

*IMPLEMENTING
A TRIP*

CHAPTER 4

PREPARING FOR COMPLEXITY

CULTURE AT WORK

It was the early 1990s. The advent of the Internet and email promised to change the way business and communication happened. At the time, I (Steve) was working in the international office of a Christian relief and development agency. My colleagues and I all expected email to make our work easier, quickly connecting us with people across the globe.

One day, I sat down to write an email to an Asian brother in Christ working in one of our country offices. In our last face-to-face interaction, we were working through an issue and had some important differences of opinion. Hoping to move forward, I thought I would clarify our positions. I typed up what I believed his perspective to be, my own opinion on the subject, and the pros and cons of each. Then I hit send, not thinking twice about what I had just done.

A few weeks later, I heard that he and his core staff were in an uproar, deeply angered and offended. Because we did not see each other often, I could not repair the breach quickly. And I certainly could not send another email, given that my first had triggered such a response. I attempted to work through appropriate intermediaries to solve our conflict. Unfortunately, there was little response from my brother.

Two years later, we were at a staff conference together. His assistant came up to me and asked me to follow her. She led me to his room and then simply left. He initiated casual small talk, and we had a lighthearted conversation as if nothing had happened. In the midst of our chat, he took out a pear native to his country, a fruit he knew I enjoyed. He began slicing it into sections, and then handed me pieces of the pear. Eventually, he looked me in the eye and nodded his head ever so slightly. I said nothing, simply receiving the pear. When I left the room, his assistant was beaming as she asked, "Is everything okay?" I smiled and said, "Yes," relief and joy overwhelming me.

I was raised in rural Vermont. From the context of my culture and upbringing, this story makes zero sense. Why the extreme reaction to the email? What was with the pear? And what did the nod mean? Deep, powerful cultural dynamics were at play—dynamics I was still coming to understand even after years of working internationally.

MORE THAN MEETS THE EYE

Visiting a low-income community requires a particularly acute awareness of cultural issues, whether we are traveling internationally or domestically. But culture is more than the clothes or food of a particular region. Culture includes deeply engrained behaviors people hold from the day they are born. These cultural norms are a subconscious set of assumptions and protocols that people naturally follow without even thinking about them. In fact, most people only become aware of cultural norms when they enter a place or a situation where people do not act the way they expect them to act. It is only then that the realization sets in: there is something significant happening beneath the surface of even seemingly mundane interactions like sending an email or sharing a pear.

Before entering the world of cultural norms, it is important to note that God gave humans creativity and the high calling of creating culture. Thus, though the fall marred aspects of all cultures, *culture is good, and the diversity of culture reflects the diversity of the people of God—and of God Himself, as three-in-one.* As a result, we are called to both appreciate and critique culture, including our own. Unfortunately, when we encounter things that are different or confusing, we tend to judge them negatively. Moving past this impulse is the first step in exploring the richness and beauty of culture.

It is impossible to explore the depths of culture in the space of a chapter. However, there are a few key cultural norms that you will encounter during a short-term trip. Even if you are not traveling internationally, keep these cultural differences in mind. Many parts of the United States, or even neighborhoods within cities, are culturally very different from churches that commonly send teams.

For simplicity's sake, this chapter is organized based on each norm, its extremes, and how the norms may work themselves out on a trip. But be aware that this chapter paints in broad brushstrokes. Describing Africa as generally polychronic, for example, is not meant to imply that African culture is monolithic. A few pages can hold only so much detail.

CONCEPT OF TIME: WHAT IS TIME, AND HOW IS IT USED?

Most trip-sending churches operate from a *monochronic* view of time, seeing time as a commodity and a limited resource to be carefully stewarded. Efficiency and productivity are primary values in monochronic cultures, as are orderliness and planning for the future.

In contrast, many low-income communities are *polychronic*, viewing time as a more expansive, nebulous, and almost limitless entity. Efficiency and punctuality are not high priorities, because there is always more time to get things done. Polychronic people do not talk about wasting time and saving time. When they see Scripture talk about "redeeming the time," they do not immediately think of creating a to-do list and hurriedly tackling it. Instead, they tend to think more of investing in relationships—not tasks—through time.

Concept of Time

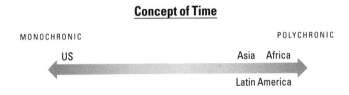

Adapted from Craig Storti, *Figuring Foreigners Out: A Practical Guide* (Yarmouth, ME: Intercultural Press, 1999), 82.

CONCEPT OF TIME AND TRIPS

By their very nature, the brevity of short-term trips intensifies monochronic Christians' emphasis on time. When teams come from a monochronic culture, they are intent on completing their objectives in that time. Phrases such as, "We've got to serve these people well—let's get this done and not waste this opportunity," roll off the tongue frequently and naturally. If a team is visiting people who are more polychronic, at some point in the trip it is likely that members of the host community will be late for an event or materials will not be delivered when they are supposed to be.

In these scenarios, monochronic people face a tempting explanation: "Clearly people here don't care about their communities or their families enough, because obviously if they did they would drop everything and would work alongside us to get this task done and completed while we're here. They have this opportunity and all of this extra help, and they are wasting it."

Meanwhile, polychronic nationals might have a different perspective: "They can't be coming here primarily to get a task done. That doesn't make sense. If they were primarily concerned about digging a well, building schools, or even having a really good VBS—if that's what they wanted then they wouldn't have spent thousands and thousands of dollars on travel and accommodations to come here. We could do those tasks more appropriately and cheaply. They must be here for a different reason. Maybe they've come here to connect with us more deeply. But then why are they in such a rush? And then why do they head out every night and go somewhere else to eat and sleep? Let's spend more time being together, talking together, sharing together, praying together, and reading the Word together."

Without cultural awareness, both sides might be confused, left with negative explanations for the other's actions and intentions.

CONCEPT OF SELF: WHAT IS "SELF"?

In highly *individualistic* cultures, such as most trip-sending churches, people celebrate the individual and freedom of choice. Everybody is different, and success is found in people "being all they can be" and being "true to oneself." As a result, there is not an acute sense of pre-set obligations or roles in life. For example, being the oldest son or the youngest daughter does not entail a stringent set of expectations and duties. Christians in individualistic cultures are concerned with discovering their unique spiritual gifts and finding their ministry calling.

Further, relationships tend to be portable in individualistic cultures: people form and leave friendships behind as life requires. Individualistic people may have childhood friends, but when they move away or change as a person, they tend to develop new sets of friends. Friends are fairly easily made and fairly easily left behind because relationships serve the purpose of a particular season or point in time.

When I am teaching about the deep and unavoidable impact of culture, I find it interesting that Westerners, especially young Americans, want to reject the notion that they are highly individualistic. They squirm in their seats, insisting, "I'm not like that, I'm different." In reality, the very fact that they do not want to be labeled as part of a larger group or collective norm further points to their extreme individualism.

In contrast to this discomfort with conformity, people from *collectivist* cultures identify themselves primarily as a member of a group, typically a family, role in society, or geographic area. Many low-income communities are also more collectivist than individualistic. In these cultures, success comes from knowing one's role in the group and fulfilling that role well. As a result, there are preset obligations, roles, and pathways placed on group members by others, especially by leaders.

Questions such as, "If I go to college, what should I major in?" or "Whom should I marry?" would never be seen as individual choices. Interdependence within the group, rather than independence and autonomy, is a core value. Christians in collectivist societies are particularly aware of their identity as part of the local church and the worldwide body of Christ.

In individualistic cultures, it is common to praise the individual and talk about his or her accomplishments. In a collectivist culture, doing so would bring shame on the person. An old Japanese proverb even says, "The nail that sticks up will be pounded down." Singling out a person for praise is inappropriate, because any success should be seen as a group effort; if an individual person is elevated, it violates the value and importance of the larger group.

Promoting group harmony is a central value in collectivism. Because members are part of groups for long periods of time, and in some cases even their entire lives, maintaining harmonious, reconciled relationships is the key to stability and success. Thus, in a collectivist society, friendships are not primarily based on emotional connectedness—the need for harmony and unity trumps individual feelings.

In *African Friends and Money Matters*, David Maranz explains that harmony, as opposed to emotional connection, is at the basis of friendship in collectivist societies partly because of the need for financial interdependence and reciprocity.[1] Being friends and part of a group means being willing to share resources. When someone lacks financial resources, others help, knowing that the group will one day be there for them in their time of need. As a result, money is very fluid within groups. The idea of saving for retirement, for example, would seem irrational in a collectivist society—belonging to the group is like an IRA or 401K. Social networks and relationships, rather than institutions, are the source of stability.

Concept of Self

Adapted from Craig Storti, *Figuring Foreigners Out: A Practical Guide* (Yarmouth, ME: Intercultural Press, 1999), 52.

CONCEPT OF SELF AND TRIPS

These differences in notions of identity and belonging can have huge implications for a trip. Americans can walk away from a visit thinking, "Wow, look at the friends that I made. We cannot speak the same language, but the Holy Spirit connected us in deep ways." Yes, precious connections happen within the body of Christ through cross-cultural engagement, but be careful before invoking the label of "friendship." In a collectivist culture, friendship involves deep obligation. When a trip participant attempts to befriend someone from a collectivist culture, they often unintentionally communicate, "I will provide for you, I will be part of your social network that involves economic interdependence." Without realizing it, participants can end up in a type of patronage system. Especially since teams are often very wealthy in contrast to the receiving community, members of the collectivist culture might expect participants to contribute significantly to their financial well-being, creating a minefield of dangerous opportunities for unhealthy giving and dependency.

LOCUS OF CONTROL: WHAT CHANGE IS POSSIBLE?

The norm of locus of control defines where people perceive the center of control in their lives to be. Cultures marked by an *internal locus of control* view themselves as being fundamentally in control of, and therefore responsible for, their lives. The vast majority of short-term teams come from these contexts. Problems can be fixed. Progress is inevitable. Obstacles exist to be overcome. In contrast, cultures with a strong sense of *external locus of control*, including many low-income communities, assume that life is complex, with interwoven, external forces at play that are not easily understood or overcome. Life is more about accepting things that cannot be controlled and understood, rather than fighting against the inevitable and unchangeable.

People from external locus of control cultures consider themselves realistic, looking at people with an internal locus of control as being very naive. In contrast, people from an internal locus of control context view themselves as proactive, perceiving external locus of control cultures as fatalistic.

Locus of Control

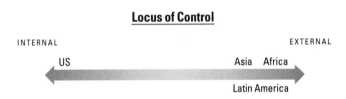

Adapted from Craig Storti, *Figuring Foreigners Out: A Practical Guide* (Yarmouth, ME: Intercultural Press, 1999), 82.

LOCUS OF CONTROL AND TRIPS

Teams from internal locus of control cultures are tempted to enter a community with ideas and dreams about how to make life better for the residents. "What if we built an irrigation system?" If they encounter resistance, they often assume the community lacks the initiative to improve its circumstances, developing a negative attitude toward the residents. In contrast, members of an external locus of control culture can become frustrated with teams' attempts to address complex problems. This understanding of control—what's possible and what isn't?—becomes a core source of tension, particularly in long-term partnerships between congregations. (This dynamic is explored more deeply in chapter 5.)

POWER DISTANCE: INTERACTING WITH AUTHORITY

Power distance describes the appropriate relationship between those who are in authority and those under authority. *Low power distance* cultures, like that of many short-term teams, believe in a more democratic style of management and decision making. Those who formally have a position of authority should treat their subordinates as if they have good ideas and are free to share those ideas. Delegation of authority is seen as beneficial and mature; there is give-and-take between bosses and subordinates, and it is possible to disagree with authority figures in an appropriate way.

High power distance cultures, however, expect people who have power to use it fully and completely. Subordinates expect to be micromanaged. In fact, they may even *want* to be micromanaged because the person in authority is assumed to know what is best. Subordinates feel safe and protected by this type of management style; they want to know what the authority figure expects, and then they execute. Disagreeing with a boss or authority figure is disgraceful, particularly in a public environment like a meeting.

Power Distance

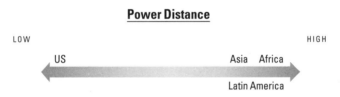

Adapted from Craig Storti, *Figuring Foreigners Out: A Practical Guide* (Yarmouth, ME: Intercultural Press, 1999), 140.

POWER DISTANCE AND TRIPS

Short-term teams, generally coming from low power distance cultures, must be particularly careful to honor and respect local leadership when entering a high power distance culture. For example, the pastor of a church in a high power distance culture is a key decision maker. This is true whether in a Latino church in inner-city Dallas, an African-American church in rural Mississippi, or a church in Rwanda. Thus, teams must work through local authority figures and not around them. Further, it is important for the formal team leader to engage in any dialogue or decision making with local authorities. Generally speaking, teams must guard against their tendency toward informality with authority figures.

However, there is an even more complicated dynamic at work. Middle-class Americans, by virtue of their wealth, are sometimes granted the status of being on the top of the power hierarchy while they are present—even surpassing local authority figures. Therefore, people from a high power distance culture may not disagree with what the team wants, especially if the team leader expresses a desire or idea. Team members can misread this compliance as assent that the team's plans are best. In reality, community members may choose not to openly disagree with the outsiders' proposed solutions, even though they doubt those solutions will work. This is another reason trips entering high power distance cultures must be very cautious not to take the reins of decision making, both in pre-trip planning and in daily interactions on the field, even if these reins are offered. It is tragic if, as relatively affluent believers, team members' economic power and privilege undermine the voices and expertise of their brothers and sisters. If local people constantly defer to outsiders' opinions or authority, something unhealthy is happening beneath the surface.

FACE: PROTECTING HONOR

"Face" is a person's reputation in a social setting or context. *High face* cultures, known as face-saving or honor and shame societies, are often collectivist cultures because harmony is a central element to long-term, interdependent relationships. Due to this dynamic, high face cultures tend to be very indirect in their communication style. In indirect cultures, "yes" often means, "I've heard you," "maybe," and in some situations, even "no." In cultures that communicate indirectly, people do not overtly say what they mean. Rather, they use ambiguous speech, often found in the form of qualifiers. Indirect communicators tend to tell stories and use parables and proverbs, and they would seldom say no to somebody publicly.

Most trip-sending churches are part of *low face* cultures. Preserving face is not as important, and respecting someone still allows for very direct communication. They say "yes" to indicate assent and "no" to communicate lack of assent. "Laying your cards on the table" is an expected part of solving problems. In high face cultures, "laying your cards on the table" is disastrous. In fact, putting disagreements in written form is offensive—it makes them more real and harsh, losing face for everyone.

A huge amount of cultural conflict occurs because of these different concepts of face and their corresponding communication styles. Direct communicators are taught to use the active tense in their speech. "I dropped the ball," for example, clearly connects the actor and the action. Indirect cultures use the passive tense frequently, i.e., "the ball dropped." The audience in an indirect culture would understand that the person speaking dropped the ball based on the context, but they would never say that directly; they distance the actor from the actions because that is a way of gently dealing with issues. People from direct cultures have a difficult time accepting this, as it seems like a way of avoiding responsibility. However, as Duane Elmer explains in *Cross-Cultural Conflict: Building Relationships for Effective Ministry*:

> When an indirect method of handling conflict is used, the Westerner often misinterprets this as (1) lack of courage to confront the person, (2) unwillingness to deal with the issue, (3) lack of commitment to solve the problem, or (4) refusal to take responsibility for one's actions. In fact, the person may be displaying both courage and commitment, but in ways that are not understood by those of us who come from a culture that values directness.[2]

In contrast, indirect cultures view direct communication as rude and immature. From their perspective, it disrupts relationships and harmony, making direct communicators untrustworthy.

Saving Face

Adapted from Craig Storti, *Figuring Foreigners Out: A Practical Guide* (Yarmouth, ME: Intercultural Press, 1999), 98.

Degree of Directness

Adapted from Craig Storti, *Figuring Foreigners Out: A Practical Guide* (Yarmouth, ME: Intercultural Press, 1999), 99.

FACE AND TRIPS

People from indirect cultures, including many low-income communities, may carefully say things that teams want to hear in order to avoid shaming their guests. If you ask an indirect communicator whether your trip was helpful, they will say yes without hesitating. Being direct about their position would be inappropriate unless they had a deep, long-term relationship with you. Instead, they will typically communicate, "Thank you for coming. This trip has been a wonderful thing for our community and we hope you will do it again." Saying anything else would cause you shame, and to cause somebody else shame would be to cause themselves shame.

I have had multiple conversations with people from indirect cultures with whom—over many years—I have become good friends. We have come to a point where we can talk more directly because they consider me part of their group. As a result, I have been able to ask them questions about how they view short-term trips. Some of the things they share are difficult to hear. But they do not want to dishonor teams, and therefore themselves, by sharing their concerns directly.

We, as leaders, have a responsibility to acknowledge this dynamic. We need to stop automatically taking praise for our trips at face value and thinking we have been so positively received. I have had to personally do this in my own work internationally. The accolades often sound strong and positive. But I have had to learn, and continue to learn, to read between the lines, determining what is just good face-saving communication.

DIFFERENCE WITHIN THE EXTREME: TRIPS IN THE UNITED STATES

As the spectrums and scenarios above demonstrate, US culture generally tends to be a bit unusual. It is typically on one of the extremes of the cultural norm continuums. Teams, when coming from US contexts, will see reality very differently from most of the people who walk this planet. However, incredible cultural variation exists within the United States. These differences are particularly strong across communities with varying ethnic and historical identities. C. E. Elliott's research in "Cross-Cultural Communication Styles" provides helpful descriptions of communication patterns in US groups and communities, including Hispanic Americans, Asian Americans, European Americans, Native Americans, and African Americans.[3]

In the case of groups such as Latino Americans and Asian Americans, cultural patterns *loosely* parallel those of their countries of origin. Short-term teams traveling to African-American communities, though, need to be particularly careful when navigating cultural differences. George Henderson's *Our Souls to Keep*, particularly chapter 3, contains helpful insights for European-American teams when entering African-American communities.[4] While all cultures are layered and nuanced, many historical, economic, and social factors have contributed to unique combinations of cultural norms and behaviors in African-American communities.[5]

- Generally speaking, African-American communities tend to be more polychronic and lean toward an external locus of control.[6]

- African-American culture exhibits collectivist tendencies; ties and harmony among family, friends, and community are extremely important. However, African Americans also operate from individualism as a norm in some settings. Individual expression and collective harmony are both key values. Even more than in other cultural groups, individualism and collectivism are not tidy, mutually exclusive categories.[7]

- Methods of communication change depending on the identity of the parties involved. African Americans tend toward greater directness with each other than with outsiders, particularly European Americans.[8]

SO WHAT?

As Americans, in particular, we often think that we are sophisticated at adapting to culture because we are a multiethnic, multicultural nation. But in the rest of the world, we are actually known as somewhat naïve, or even provincial, in our ability to navigate culture. Europeans and Canadians, who are much more interculturally competent than we are, look at us and shake their heads at our self-delusions.

In contrast, many receiving communities have had to interact with affluent US culture because of its power, wealth, and presence, and are thus proficient at adjusting to it. Their adaptability can make trips seem smoother. However, we have to recognize and appreciate that people are bending to us, helping ease our interactions and presence in their communities. They are integrating to our culture, even as we enter their world. *We are the visitors, and yet the home team is doing most of the adjusting.* What does it mean to consider others' interests more important than our own as we enter another culture? It is time for us to stop merely enjoying the benefits of others accommodating our culture. We need to learn to respect others and play by their cultural rules.

MOVING FORWARD

Outsiders cannot interpret and understand all that is happening in a given situation. But it is all too easy to create conflict. Thus, part of preparing for a visit is learning to be more interculturally competent, or as some people describe it, more "culturally intelligent." In *Serving with Eyes Wide Open: Doing Short-Term Missions with Cultural Intelligence,* David Livermore presents an excellent introduction to STMs and issues of cultural awareness. The chapters on the way many Majority World Christians see issues such as biblical training, money, and commitment versus how American Christians see them are priceless. At minimum, every leader on a team should read it.

In addition, read at least the first five chapters of Elmer's *Cross-Cultural Conflict* and consider also reading *Cross-Cultural Servanthood*.[9] In a detailed and accessible way, Elmer explores the dynamics that occur when high and low face cultures meet, provides practical insights about those tensions and miscommunications and how to navigate them, and describes what effectively loving our brothers and sisters looks like.

One last thing to remember about cross-cultural engagement via trips: it is easy to overstate the level of cultural understanding that occurs in the space of two weeks. It takes years to fully realize the depths of cultural differences—let alone appreciate or adapt to them. Thus, as always, humbly working through good partners and hosts is key in both navigating culture and learning to be more culturally appropriate.

THE CASE OF THE EMAIL AND THE PEAR

Becoming more culturally intelligent has certainly been a process in my life—I have made my share of mistakes, as the story at the beginning of this chapter illustrates. There were a number of ways differing cultural norms shaped my experience with my Asian brother. First, I (Steve) tried to directly communicate my concerns and thoughts to someone from a highly indirect culture, and even went so far as to put my concerns in writing. Second, because his office was also in a collectivist culture and I had shamed their leader, other staff felt shamed and angry. I had caused him to lose face, and thus insulted the others, as well.

But cultural norms also informed our reconciliation. I knew directly addressing the offense would only do more harm, particularly if I put anything in writing again. But when he sliced that pear, and when I accepted that pear, we both were clearly, tangibly reconciling with one another. He was apologizing for his harsh response of anger and refusing to have the conflict mediated. No words about our disagreement were ever spoken. But repentance happened clearly through the pear and the nod, and we were able to then move forward in enjoying the benefits of reconciliation.

Cross-cultural interaction is a rich, beautiful process, when done conscientiously and with plenty of grace. When the body of Christ joins together, respecting and appreciating one another's differences, we demonstrate the unity and love that flows from the work of Christ in our lives. The next chapter will unpack how these cultural dynamics, dynamics that are powerful even in a one-week visit, can become fundamental when forming long-term partnerships with people of different cultural and socioeconomic backgrounds.

TAKEAWAYS

- Cultural dynamics are a core aspect of the success and failure of a trip.

- The culture of many middle-class, trip-sending churches is "weird" compared to the rest of the world. Be humble about that reality, and expect misunderstandings.

- Trip leaders *must* be culturally competent people.

- While reading won't solve every cross-cultural tension, commit to reading *at least* David Livermore's *Serving with Eyes Wide Open* and the first five chapters of Duane Elmer's *Cross-Cultural Conflict*.

CHAPTER 5

DANCING WELL

IDENTIFYING HOSTS AND EXPLORING PARTNERSHIPS

Implementing visits focused on learning, fellowship, and encouragement requires humbly partnering with organizations and ministries working in low-income communities. Missions expert Miriam Adeney relates a story told to her by an African Christian friend that highlights the need for conscientious partnerships:

> Elephant and Mouse were best friends. One day Elephant said, "Mouse, let's have a party!" Animals gathered from far and near. They ate, and drank, and sang, and danced. And nobody celebrated more exuberantly than the Elephant. After it was over, Elephant exclaimed, "Mouse, did you ever go to a better party? What a celebration!" But Mouse did not answer. "Where are you?" Elephant called. Then he shrank back in horror. There at his feet lay the Mouse, his body ground into the dirt—smashed by the exuberance of his friend, the Elephant. "Sometimes that is what it is like to do mission with you Westerners," the African storyteller commented. "It is like dancing with an Elephant."[1]

Working with good partners is both a dance in and of itself *and* a way of seeking to dance well with the broader community in which those partners minister. Different models of sending short-term trips and establishing partnerships present unique opportunities and challenges as we—with our very large feet—seek to tread carefully.

This chapter has two basic purposes: The first is to explore the process of identifying a field partner for a healthy trip to a materially poor community. The second is to introduce how such trips might be part of establishing and maintaining long-term, formal partnerships with select field partners in order to jointly pursue ministry together across time. In both scenarios, the trip participants will be partaking in the long-term process of learning in order to move toward more purposeful participation in the work of poverty alleviation over the course of their lives. The difference is whether or not the trip itself is part of forming or cultivating an institutional partnership in which your church will link arms with a church or organization in the low-income community, jointly engaging in ministry on an ongoing basis. In addition, this chapter will discuss several ways to pursue each of these two options. Hence, as you read this chapter, carefully consider which approach best fits your church's ministry goals and capacity.

WHITHER, WHERE, WHENCE?—IDENTIFYING A VISIT PARTNER

One relatively easy approach for your church to pursue is using a well-respected intermediary to connect your church to an effective poverty alleviation ministry that is working in a low-income community. For example, many Christian relief and development organizations act as intermediaries, connecting North American churches to their ministries in low-income communities in the Majority World. The intermediary can link your church to field staff who are prepared to complete much of the logistical planning of the trip, to provide region-specific resources as your team completes pre-trip learning, and to facilitate healthy interactions with staff and the people in the community. In essence, the intermediary pairs you with a ministry in a community, prepares you to dance well, and then guides your interactions, seeking to ensure that you do not trample "mouse" at the proverbial party.

A good intermediary will also have established methods of on- and post-field learning and engagement for team members, thereby deepening their understanding of and engagement in quality poverty alleviation work. They will have tested these methods already, ensuring that these mechanisms do not create dependency or undermine the initiative of the community. While there may be some community-initiated work in which teams can participate while on the field, a good intermediary will be focused on supporting the local staff as they engage in the long-term process of asset-based, participatory development. And a good intermediary will embrace the idea that the primary goal for the trip participants is to engage in learning, encouragement, and fellowship (see chapter 3).

The larger and more experienced the intermediary is, the more set in stone potential types of involvement will be; it will not be worth their time to adapt to what your team might want to see happen on your visit. Making constant exceptions and modifications for individual teams and churches is not good stewardship of their resources. If you enter into a long-term partnership as described below, you may be able to open up a dialogue about exploring slightly different options. In contrast, smaller or younger intermediaries may be more open to discussing what a visit might look like; however, they may not be as skilled at handling the logistics as the larger organizations. Either way, the existence of an intermediary organization provides structure and reduces the amount of work required of your church and team leaders.

Whether you are considering a trip through an intermediary or directly connecting to a ministry in the field, the first questions are always whether the staff on the ground would like to receive a team and whether they are engaged in healthy, asset-based, participatory poverty alleviation work. Here are some additional things to consider:

- Do all the parties involved support a visit from a team that is focused on learning, fellowship, and encouragement, or do they insist that the focus be on "doing"?

- When considering how the team will spend its time on the field, are there numerous and extended opportunities planned for team members to hear from field staff and from church and community leaders and members? If not, would the organization be willing to create these opportunities for your team?

- Will the community be prepped to know that the team is not primarily coming to do a particular work project or to lead a set of activities?

- Will the team have an opportunity to add their labor or participation to an existing, locally initiated project that will be carried out by the members of the local church or community?

- Will the team be given ideas for what future positive engagement could look like?

- Will an adequate number of competent translators and local staff members be available to facilitate your time in the community?

- Can the team eat with and stay in the community during the visit? If so, will adjustments be made to promote the safety and health of participants?

Finding answers to these questions, while potentially time-consuming, will help you identify a good partner for a visit. Some organizations will be caught off-guard by these types of questions, as they do not fit what many teams have historically been looking for in a trip. But some organizations will be interested, especially if they sense that there are growing numbers of teams looking for the different approach described in this book. Indeed, part of shifting the STM movement is freeing and encouraging intermediary agencies to provide visit options with a learning and engagement focus. Be both humble and bold, giving organizations a reason and space to offer a different sort of trip.

FORMING LONG-TERM PARTNERSHIPS USING INTERMEDIARIES

Your church can also use intermediaries to facilitate long-term partnerships with ministries in low-income communities, or it can choose to partner directly with ministries in materially poor communities. Trips can then help to initiate and to maintain these partnerships. Be open to this possibility, as long-term partnerships, when done well, can lead to incredible, sustained change on both sides of the equation.

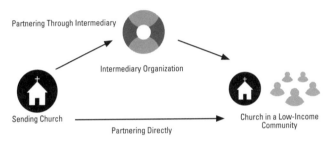

Creating a long-term partnership via an intermediary organization entails many of the same dynamics as utilizing one to mediate a single field visit. The intermediary will have established policies for forming partnerships and for appropriate ways to engage, possibly including opportunities for joint prayer and worship, financially supporting projects, sharing in ministry, and regular visits.

If you prove to be a faithful, humble partner, there may be an opportunity to seek some adaptation in the form of partnership. For example, an intermediary might have initially requested your church to sponsor a certain number of children in a community. Over time, you might approach the intermediary about providing funding for additional staff members to work in the context of those programs instead of expanding your involvement through sponsoring more children. The additional field staff might allow the work to address deeper aspects of families and communities than child sponsorship could on its own.

As is the case with single visits, seeking a long-term partnership with a smaller intermediary might allow more freedom to shape your church's involvement. But it might also require more time and effort. Again, if your church does not have extensive experience in partnerships, do not underestimate the work and wisdom involved. Partnering through a more established intermediary could be a good first step.

FORMING LONG-TERM PARTNERSHIPS DIRECTLY

Direct congregation-to-congregation or congregation-to-ministry partnerships can be powerful vehicles for transformation. But recognize that this approach will put a greater burden on you to navigate planning, decision making, implementing trips, and long-term collaboration. Simply put, unless a church is very experienced, forming partnerships directly provides more opportunities for our elephant-sized feet to cause damage. We can create conflict, cause discouragement, and be a poor witness in the community.

But when done well, members of both the sending church and the receiving church and community can get to know one another deeply and to understand each other's lives and stories more fully. Effective direct partnerships demonstrate and promote unity in the body of Christ and speak powerfully of our love for one another, testifying that Jesus Christ is Lord sent by our heavenly Father (John 17:20–21).

Direct, long-term partnerships require even more sensitivity to cultural differences than a short-term trip. Differences in cultural norms will arise with respect to shame and honor, direct and indirect forms of communication, notions of success, the appropriate pace of progress, and respective roles. The danger of misunderstanding each other and judging each other is enormous, and it typically takes *years* to develop a real foundation of trust.

To complicate things even more, people from high shame cultures often will not share their frustrations and disagreements quickly or directly, as we saw in chapter 4. They may choose to tolerate an unhealthy situation, which is a tragic scenario, particularly within the body of Christ. These issues of cultural competence can be overcome, but be aware of the potential dangers and costs. It takes immense patience and restraint to avoid undermining the leadership and initiative of the local community, and it requires constant humility to recognize and adjust our behaviors when we inadvertently strain the partnership.

Again, David Livermore's *Serving with Eyes Wide Open* and Duane Elmer's *Cross-Cultural Conflict* are essential resources in navigating these tensions.

One key question in direct partnerships is determining what type of short-term visit will be the most helpful. Depending on the context, an initial lay learning trip, which is the primary focus of this *Leader's Guide* and the companion *Participant's Guide*, may provide the catalyst that leads to a deeper partnership. Smaller, strategic partnership trips will then need to happen to explore opportunities for collaboration. Strategic partnership trips will entail a series of visits ensuring that a sense of mutuality and interdependence is established in culturally appropriate ways. They can then provide the basis for further lay learning trips, if the receiving ministry feels that lay groups could be incorporated healthily and effectively.

A short chapter cannot be an exhaustive exploration of developing and maintaining healthy direct partnerships. Thankfully, many brothers and sisters have already created excellent resources to assist churches in this process. While some of these resources focus on connecting Western churches with Majority World churches, the principles, practices, and tools presented are equally valuable for partnerships between churches and ministries within the US.

Here are a few resources you should consider utilizing:

- **Materials from Daniel Rickett**: Some of the best ideas and principles for partnership come from the work of Daniel Rickett. He has written important books on partnership, including *Making Your Partnership Work: A Guide for Ministry Leaders* and *Building Strategic Relationships: A Practical Guide to Partnering with Non-Western Missions.*[2] His website, www.danielrickett.com, is loaded with practical resources and tools. You will want to utilize these early and often. Furthermore, his organization offers consulting if you would like to pursue healthy partnerships.

- **Coalition on the Support of Indigenous Ministries**: COSIM is a network of people and organizations that have long been engaged in cross-cultural partnership. Their website, www.cosim. info, is a treasure trove of information.

• ***The Beauty of Partnership***: A study guide created by Mission ONE and edited by Werner Mischke, this six-week course is a good starting point for moving into cross-cultural partnerships.[3]

FOUR COMMUNITIES, TWO STORIES

So what is the potential of a healthy long-term partnership, whether through an intermediary or via a direct relationship?

Ryan is a lay leader in a US church. Working through an intermediary that supports effective, community-led development work, Ryan's church is in the midst of a six-year commitment with a community in Africa. Local leaders identified and initiated projects to improve the life of the community, such as purchasing schoolbooks, constructing a school, and digging a well. The intermediary plugged Ryan's church into supporting those needs in a healthy manner. Ryan explains, "Ten-year olds at our church helped raise money to supplement what the community was already investing in digging a well. . . . and then a team from our church traveled to see and contribute to the work. When we got there, we were massively outnumbered by community members who came to execute the project." Through partnering with this intermediary and community over years, the number of students in the African community passing the high school entry test has jumped 300–400 percent.[4]

In the early 1990s, several people from Jason's community in the US developed relationships with leaders in a low-income community abroad. They became involved in ministry and medical service in local orphanages, and working directly with ministry partners over the years, have supported and worked to arrange stable homes and living conditions for the children. In addition to carefully supporting effective ministry in the low-income community, Jason and his fellow community members have developed relationships with the children and teenagers. Team members meet year round, studying Scripture together, learning their brothers and sisters' language, and praying for them. Jason shares, "Every year, the youth in our community and the youth in the community abroad choose a 'spiritual formation theme' that they want to study and explore together. We study the same things and share our reflections with each other via video chat and during our time on the field. We have studied themes like grace, hospitality, leadership—we are always learning from them."[5] Through these visits and partnership, deep learning, encouragement, engagement, and effective ministry are flourishing.

The following chapters will dig deeper into what it means to dance well during visits themselves, respecting partners and community members on the field. But for now, carefully consider how trips fit within your church's approach to ministry and poverty alleviation.

TAKEAWAYS

- Decide whether you will be engaging in a short-term trip via an intermediary or via a direct contact, considering the different levels of work required for each.

- Ensure that any organization you work with provides extensive learning and fellowship opportunities with local staff, leaders, and community and church members.

- Before creating or deepening a long-term, direct partnership, be sure appropriate church leaders have investigated some of the resources described in this chapter in order to get a clearer idea of what being a good partner entails and costs.

- If exploring potential long-term partnership opportunities, whether through an intermediary or directly, be sure that appropriate church decision makers are part of the trip.

CHAPTER 6

OVERCOMING INERTIA

APPLYING A
DIFFERENT FRAMEWORK

In 1687, Isaac Newton described his first law of motion, a concept we simply know as *inertia*. A ball rolling on a frictionless plane without any physical or gravitational interference would roll indefinitely, having no reason to change course. Likewise, an object launched in space, without any interrupting outside forces, would travel forever on the same trajectory.

Any ministry leader—with or without a background in physics—will tell you that inertia exists within churches and organizations. Simply put, change is hard. The status quo will continue in churches' practices and attitudes until acted upon by some force.

It is one thing to personally accept and move toward a new framework of what short-term trips should be. But overcoming the institutional inertia created by tradition, sentiment, and good intentions is a different ball game. Church leaders in the midst of this transition share a common refrain: *I'm on board, but my missions committee isn't. Our congregation has been collecting school supplies for materially poor children and rehabbing houses every summer for ten years. I've tried speaking up, pointing out the unintended harm we may be causing, and people look at me like I don't care about missions and people who are poor. What should I do?*

Ultimately, the Holy Spirit has to show up and change a church, re-working the hearts of both leaders and congregation members toward a healthier understanding of His mission and their role in it. Constantly pray that He would act, giving everyone soft hearts, wisdom, and perseverance. But some concrete ways are available for leaders to move toward a healthier trip framework in their ministries and congregations. It is messy, but worth it.

You may or may not be able to totally remake your short-term trips and missions programs through upper-level decisions, depending on your church's culture and history. Some churches are not locked in to a particular pattern of STMs and can change direction fairly quickly, even though it is still painful. Others have a long history of taking particular trips and engaging in certain types of activities, making change a much more grueling process.

Most frequently, change comes in frustratingly small steps. Community development expert Roland Bunch says that the key to unleashing change in a low-income community is to "start small and succeed."[1] The same applies to a church or ministry seeking to change their approach to short-term trips.

On one level, taking a healthy trip is an opportunity to shift how participants think about the materially poor and poverty alleviation. People who engage in the long-term learning process can then become advocates for wider cultural change in your church's approach to poverty. On another level, helping your congregation to shift its thinking about the fundamental nature of poverty can prepare the congregation to accept a different type of trip. Taking healthy trips and fostering cultural change are mutually enforcing processes.

But pushing for cultural change in your church is a much bigger undertaking, and it may not be a good starting point, depending on your level of influence within the church. Thus, do not feel like you have to remake your entire church before organizing a healthy trip.

Again, "start small and succeed."

In this light, view the various suggestions in this chapter as helpful pieces of what is likely to be a long-term process of change—pieces that can be arranged and adapted for your particular context.

TALKING POVERTY

Broader conversations about poverty, specifically with your fellow church and ministry leaders, can inform *or* flow from a retooled trip. Open the dialogue informally, sharing the things you have been learning and wrestling with about the complexity of poverty alleviation. On a practical level, some pastors have shared that encouraging their staff, elders, or ministry leaders to read *When Helping Hurts* is helpful in this process.

In terms of specifically addressing short-term trips, if you have a personal relationship with people from the ministry or the community that receives your trips, *listen to their experiences*. Humbly ask them to share their perspective on your trips and work, including any ways that they have been hurt or ways they might like you to change your practices. This listening process can be complicated by the cultural differences described in chapter 4, but it is a place to start. If they are willing and able to put their thoughts in writing, ask if they would be comfortable sharing their words with the leadership of the church. It is always difficult to hear that our well-intentioned efforts may be missing the mark. But it is harder to ignore or dismiss words coming directly from the brothers and sisters we are impacting.

Educating the broader congregation about poverty alleviation can also be helpful. If your leadership team simply announces that you are overhauling your short-term trips, the congregation may not respond well. Until congregations understand that poverty is rooted in broken relationships, that poverty alleviation is a lengthy process, that they cannot "rescue" people who are poor, and that God has placed unique assets in low-income communities, moving toward an approach of learning, fellowshiping, and long-term engagement might seem like a compromise or cop-out. Consider working through *When Helping Hurts:*

The Small Group Experience in Sunday school sessions and other groups, unpacking the principles of effective poverty alleviation together.

Personal stories from people in and around the church can make the concepts of poverty alleviation more accessible. For example, within the boundaries of appropriate confidentiality, have staff or leaders within your congregation share stories about a time when they inadvertently harmed a low-income person or community. Have them reflect on what they would do differently now if they had a do-over. In a similar vein, have people share times when they approached interacting with the materially poor from a healthier, more effective framework.

If individuals in your church have personally experienced material poverty and feel safe enough to talk about those experiences, ask them to share with your congregation. Invite them to tell stories of when well-intended help actually hurt them, as well as stories of when someone's help truly benefited them.

TALKING MISSIONS

Many churches view traditional STMs as a key pillar of their missions strategy. Thus, questioning STMs is sometimes viewed as undermining commitment to missions in the broader sense. Changes to your trips may be better received if your church is proactively emphasizing the importance of long-term missions and the beautiful work God is already doing through His people around the globe. With or without a short-term trip, there are things every church and congregation member should be doing to engage with missions. As Miriam Adeney, associate professor of World Christian Studies at Seattle Pacific University, explains, "We must teach alternatives [to STMs] over and over in attractive, reasonable, convincing ways, until church members understand the value of investing prayer and money in long term love."[2] In light of Adeney's observations, consider the following suggestions:[3]

- **Highlight the work and dignity of your ministry partners.** At gatherings such as Sunday school classes, small groups, or even Sunday services, consider video chatting with a partner missionary or community development worker. Ask them to explain the work they are doing, how God is using it, and how you as a congregation can specifically pray for them. As church members see what God is already doing through His people within low-income communities, it will be harder and harder to think that they have to go "save" those communities. They will also gain a sense of the depth and breadth of that work, work that could not happen through a ten-day trip.

- **Enter into your partners' worlds.** Provide your congregation or network with updates about the political, social, and spiritual context of your partners' work. If you partner with a ministry in inner-city Detroit, take time to explain how high unemployment is shaping their outreach efforts. If you support a church-equipping agency in the Middle East, keep your congregation educated on the general causes of unrest in places like Syria, explaining how the resulting refugee crisis is creating both challenges and opportunities for their ministry. If possible, read updates on these issues from your local contacts, or ask them to explain these issues in a video chat. As the complexity of your partners' worlds becomes more apparent, the expectation that short-term trips will dramatically change those worlds will diminish.

- **Create consistent time to pray for missions.** Rather than taking time once a year for Missions Week, make praying for the specific requests of your ministry partners a frequent part of your worship services or meetings.

- **Unpack the benefits of long-term engagement.** As your congregation grows in its understanding of the work God is doing, explain the importance of engaging deeply and consistently with a few organizations or partners over time, thus supporting lasting change in low-income communities. Explain that the work local ministries are doing is made possible by steady, patient investment, and that any short-term visits are only one piece of engaging in that work.

Implementing these types of suggestions situates your church and short-term trips in the context of already-existing, long-term work. It also begins the process of presenting encouragement, learning, and fellowship as legitimate forms of engaging with missions, reinforcing a healthy approach to trips.

TO GO OR NOT TO GO

Prayerfully work with your fellow leaders to discern what role short-term visits have in your missions approach. Consider the opportunity cost and stewardship questions: Is this how God would have you use His resources? If so, on what scale? Do you have people in your congregation who would be truly committed to the learning and long-term engagement process, making the use of these resources more worthwhile? Are you, as leaders, committed to doing the work of preparing the team and coordinating the contextual, cultural, and spiritual training needed to go as learners? Or is a strategic partnership trip a more appropriate fit, rather than taking a learning trip with lay church members? These are weighty questions, and they require prayer, discussion, and wisdom.

If you decide to move forward with a trip, there is another question you must ask: *has one of your ministry partners requested a team, or do you have an opportunity to go through an intermediary that is placing teams as requested?* Remember: it is impossible to take a healthy trip without local initiation, direction, and ownership. David Livermore explains the all-too-common current reality, describing the typical conversation he has when approaching STM organizations' booths at conferences:

> I ask them how the national church is engaged in what they're doing. Consistently I hear, "Oh yes, we're very committed to working with the national churches there. We ask them if they want to be involved." Did you catch that? We ask them if *they* want to be involved. Maybe we should start by asking if *we* should be involved at all, and if so, how? What might it look like if nationals helped us open our eyes to the real needs? Not only is it colonialist to invite nationals' input on the back end of planning, but we often end up doing irrelevant and costly work.

> Local ownership . . . means letting the local churches actually direct
> and shape what we do in our cross-cultural efforts; they ask *us* if we
> want to be involved rather than vice versa.[4]

The bottom line: if you are not asked, do not go.

UNINTENDED CONSEQUENCES

Be careful if you decide the best course of action is pausing or stopping
your short-term trips. Yes, there are negative consequences of STMs
that need to be addressed, and some churches find that a reset is necessary. However, remember that part of your participant fee in the past
may have supported the long-term work of the agency or organization
with which you were partnering. If you choose to stop taking short-term
trips with a particular partner engaged in effective work, *you may be cutting
into one of their funding sources.* As a result, you need to carefully consider
how to compensate in your giving; otherwise, you have merely traded
one set of unintended consequences for another. The last thing you want
is to harm brothers and sisters who are involved in healthy poverty alleviation ministries.

Inertia is powerful, and overcoming it requires even more powerful
forces. Thankfully, the Holy Spirit, the author and instigator of change
in our hearts and our churches, is at work. God is dedicated to acting
in and through His church, and He will never give up on that project.
So take hope. Change is messy but not impossible. Take small, tangible
steps, exploring the role God has prepared for your congregation in
proclaiming and demonstrating the good news of Christ's work.

TAKEAWAYS

- If you are in a church that you feel needs to change its STMs in
  low-income communities, decide if you are going to either:
  — Organize a healthy trip as described in this guide, using it as a
    stepping-stone for conversations about poverty alleviation and
    missions in your church

— Work with appropriate church leaders to start shifting the broader culture of poverty alleviation and missions in your church, then take a trip as an outgrowth of that change

- Regardless of your answer above, take a moment to consider what connecting congregation members to missions and poverty alleviation ministries might look like in your particular context. (See suggestions in "Talking Poverty" and "Talking Missions.")

CHAPTER 7

SOME ASSEMBLY REQUIRED

BUILDING THE TEAM

Imagine that Patrick walks up to the podium, ready to announce an upcoming short-term trip to his congregation. It is the first communication he will have with the whole church about the trip, and it is the congregation's first taste of what the trip will look like.

"We will be going to the Ninth Ward in New Orleans, working with New Life Community Church to bring hope to an area that was devastated by Katrina. It's heartbreaking to think that such poverty still exists here in America—when you see it, you will have no choice but to act. This is an opportunity to get in the trenches and really help the least of these, bringing the light of the gospel to a dark area. We are blessed to live such lives of relative comfort, and sacrificing two weeks is the least we can do."

He sits back down, looking forward to talking to interested church members after the service.

Now imagine that Heather, a leader at another church that is also sending a team to New Life, has her own elevator speech to describe the very same trip. Walking up to the microphone, she begins:

"We will be visiting believers at New Life Community Church in New Orleans, a church started in the Ninth Ward after Katrina. This is an opportunity to learn about their ongoing efforts to help rebuild their community and to share the gospel following the storm. We want to get a sense of how we can best love and support them over the long haul, as well as why poverty is such a systemic issue in the area. We will have four months of pre-trip meetings, a ten-day trip, and six months of follow-up conversations as we explore the place God might have for us in supporting the work of His church in New Orleans—and in our own community."

One trip. Two very different sets of expectations.

THE EXPECTATIONS GAME

Implementing a learning and engagement approach to visits is a process, including explaining an actual trip to your congregation. Depending on your church's history, there may be moments of shock and disorientation as your congregation realizes that this trip will not be like STMs of the past.

Thus, part of moving toward a healthier framework for short-term trips involves intentionally fostering a new set of expectations in the hearts and minds of the congregation and participants before, during, and after the trip.

Brian Howell, professor of anthropology at Wheaton College, has extensively researched the development and practice of STMs, including an in-depth analysis of a trip to the Dominican Republic. In particular, he studied the role participants' expectations played in shaping how they understood their experiences. He noticed that because the trip was structured, marketed, and talked about primarily as an avenue for sacrificing for the poor, doing evangelism, and experiencing personal transformation, participants walked away with nearly uniform stories and observations that neatly fit those boxes. In other words, the expectations participants brought on the plane heavily determined what lessons they brought back. Howell even observed that the existing STM framework sometimes blinded participants to opportunities for deeper learning and change because they were focused on making what they saw fit with their expectations.[1]

If you want a different sort of trip, you have to cast a different vision, clearly articulating an alternative set of goals and outcomes.

SUPPORTIVE LEADERS

Fostering a healthy set of expectations will heavily influence the composition of your team, including the team leaders. Too often, team leaders are selected primarily because of their enthusiasm and influence within a church or ministry. On a practical level, it is difficult to tell someone who is expecting to play a particular role in a trip, "No thank you." But if you do not have team leaders who support a healthier approach to trips, the inertia of previous practices and traditions will naturally hijack the visit.

As you identify potential leaders, look for the following characteristics:[2]

- **Existing engagement in missions and poverty alleviation—or movement in that direction.** By definition, a huge part of effective leadership is modeling by example. If trip leaders are not engaged at some level in the world of missions and poverty alleviation, it will be difficult to convince participants to be.

- **Strong commitment to effective poverty alleviation principles and dedication to holding participants accountable to those principles**. As one short-term trip leader shared, "As soon as boots hit the ground and team members see the material needs around them, they are tempted to throw what they learned about the harm of handouts out the window. They want to act. They think they have the money and the ideas needed to solve the problem, but they can end up doing incredible damage to future work."[3] You and your fellow leaders have to be emotionally strong enough to hold the line, reminding participants of the principles of poverty alleviation in the midst of emotionally challenging situations.

- **Humility and willingness to submit to local leaders.** You and your leadership team must be prepared to obey the directions of local church and ministry leaders, even when doing so goes against your own preferences or what the team wants.

- **Respect from the team members.** In order to effectively guide participants and support you, leaders must have the team's respect. Look for leaders who have strong relationships within the church, and who are also strong enough to lovingly say no when they need to.

- **Experience in cross-cultural travel and/or relationships.** Look for people who understand the complexity of navigating cross-cultural settings and are willing to be flexible. Short-term trips always involve unforeseen complications. Leaders must be prepared to adapt to proverbial curveballs and help participants accept those changes with an attitude of joy and respect.

You may not have people who fit all of these qualifications, and fierce politics can exist in churches and ministries. But in the early stages of planning the trip, prayerfully ask a few people to join you as coleaders and coordinators, ensuring that you have at least some leaders who are onboard with a healthy vision for the trip.

Meet regularly with this group of people throughout the trip planning and preparation process. Pray together and rehearse how you will respond to questions or resistance you may get from participants. As a group, study the context of the community that will be receiving your team, digging deeper than the participants themselves will be able to do. If possible, spend time growing together through volunteering at a local ministry that is involved in effective poverty alleviation work and reflect together on what you observe and experience.

NOTHING IS NEUTRAL

Every time you communicate with your congregation about the visit, whether in an announcement in a Sunday service, an all-church email, or a causal conversation, ask yourself whether you are communicating a traditional STM narrative or a narrative that presents the trip as merely a piece of the long-term learning and engagement process. Use the following questions to guide your communications.

What are you communicating—explicitly or implicitly—about:

- **The desired outcome of the trip?** Are you presenting learning, fellowship, encouragement, and long-term engagement as the goals, or are you using rhetoric that communicates a focus on quickly alleviating poverty and creating a certain type of spiritual transformation?

- **The scope of the trip?** Are you clearly situating the trip as one step in an eight- to twelve-month process of intentional learning, which should in turn lead to a lifetime of engagement with missions and poverty alleviation? Or are you presenting the trip as a commodity, something to be consumed as a standalone act of service or spiritual experience?

- **The local church, believers, and the materially poor?** Are you emphasizing their assets, the gifts and strengths God has given them, or only their needs and the things they lack?

- **The potential participants?** Are you communicating that their role is to humbly learn from the materially poor community members about the complexities of their context and about what God is doing through our brothers and sisters there? Or are you painting a picture of the participants heroically serving and rescuing the materially poor?

Think back to Patrick's and Heather's announcements at the beginning of the chapter. While the intentions behind each description may be good, they create opposite expectations, preparing the congregation and the participants for drastically different experiences. The first focuses on the team members as people called to intervene in a dark, miserable place. The second focuses on understanding and supporting the work the local church and the ministries are already doing. One depicts the community as desperate for someone to "save" it. The other upholds the dignity of the community's residents and seeks to understand poverty's enduring hold in New Orleans, calling participants to consider their role in God's work.

Other details matter, too. For example, be careful what pictures you use in marketing the trip. On posters or slides, avoid images that emphasize the apparent desperation of material poverty, or that depict non-materially poor people as "saving" people who are materially poor. A picture of a hurting, vacant-eyed mother may emotionally compel people to sign up for the trip, but it undermines her dignity. An image of teenagers passing out food at a soup kitchen draws participants into a dynamic in which they expect to "rescue" people through providing material resources. It also implies that the trip will be about alleviating poverty—something you cannot directly do in the context of a short-term trip.

Likewise, be careful how you use images of children. Malnourished, needy-looking children may be effective in recruiting participants, but such pictures often establish a paternalistic narrative focused on how much outsiders have to offer the poor community. Consider using images that portray the community's strength and resilience in the midst of their poverty, rather than just their deficits.

CREATING THE TEAM

Presenting a different narrative of what your visit will be about—and the long-term commitment required—is the first step in recruiting your team. On a practical level, Ryan, a lay leader who coordinates trips at his church, has found that articulating these types of expectations directly and openly allows people to self-select based on whether or not the retooled approach is something they are willing to embrace.

> We hold a specific informational meeting where we describe how and
> why we do short-term trips differently, explaining why we don't engage
> in unhealthy giving or handout-driven activities. We provide as much

detail as we can about the trip up-front. As a result, potential team members can think through and pray through whether they are called to this opportunity, moving past just an emotional response. . . . It actually helps keep folks who maybe shouldn't go from even applying.[4]

At this type of meeting, clearly communicate what the trip will—and will not—be in terms of its purpose, activities, and goals. Preview the *Helping Without Hurting in Short-Term Missions Participant's Guide*, paying particular attention to the Learning and Engagement Agreement before unit 1. Outline the structure and frequency of the pre- and post-trip meetings your leadership has established (see chapters 8 and 9), and communicate why a degree of personal financial investment is required for participating in the trip.

There will likely still be people who want to go partially out of tradition, a desire for adventure, or a sense of spiritual duty. That is fine, to a degree, as part of the purpose of a visit is to reshape how people understand missions, poverty alleviation, and the church. But participants still need to be humble and mature enough to accept your leadership, to listen and engage in pre- and post-trip learning, and to submit to the leadership of local hosts on the field.

For those who are still interested, begin the formal application process, including an interview. Some churches also include references and short essays in the application process, though that may not be feasible for your congregation. Use whatever interview process you create to reinforce a healthy trip approach and identify areas on which you need to place a particular focus in pre-trip preparation. These interviews should not be designed as a litmus test to determine who can go; more than the "right" answers, an interview is yet another opportunity to communicate that this trip will not be the standard STM experience and that it is a learning commitment. You are looking for people who are willing to learn and grow, and an interview helps you to gain a sense of whether participants are open to that process. For example, ask questions like this in the interview:

- Why are you interested in participating in this trip? What do you hope the outcome of the trip will be?

- What do you hope to learn from this trip?

- How would you define poverty? What do you think causes poverty?

- What experience do you have in interacting with people who are materially poor?

- Are you already engaged in missions and poverty alleviation in your own community? If so, how?

- Have you ever been immersed in a culture different than your own, whether in your own city or internationally? If so, what did you learn from that experience?

- Describe a time when you submitted to authority—even though you disagreed with that authority.

- Are you willing to commit to mandatory meetings both before and after the trip? (Describe the structure and frequency of the pre- and post-trip meetings you have created. See chapters 8 and 9.)

- Are you willing to contribute a portion of your own money to the cost of the trip? (Describe the amount you are requiring participants to contribute toward the trip.)

Since the purpose of an effective visit is to learn from and encourage local believers, participants must also be emotionally resilient enough to navigate the heavy things they will encounter. A community development worker who led an anti-human trafficking initiative in Southeast Asia shared an example of what can happen when participants are not personally capable of processing the pain they witness:

> There was a short-term team that came to observe the work we were doing in caring for victims of sex trafficking after their escape. I was giving the team a tour of the facility, and a woman burst into tears right in front of a girl who had been trafficked. The experience of see-

ing the pain and injustice up close was understandably emotional. But this woman burst into hysterical crying. The little girl was confused and afraid, and she felt like a spectacle.[5]

It is impossible to predict how every participant will react to what they will likely see when visiting a low-income community. But it is important to establish parameters, particularly through age restrictions, based on the location and type of poverty you will be encountering on the field.

After the screening process, if you are truly concerned that a participant has not bought in to a learning and engagement approach, lacks the emotional maturity to navigate the experience, and cannot be sufficiently contained by the team leaders and other participants, you have a responsibility to say no to them participating. It is unfair to consciously expose the receiving community to harm for the sake of not rocking the boat in your own congregation. Yes, some people experience extreme spiritual and personal transformation through short-term trips. But hoping for such an experience at the expense of the receiving community is not "doing unto others" well.

One church leader, Mark, describes his experiences in saying no to applicants this way:

> Sometimes people want to go to escape some personal situation or to "earn" something from God. Usually those motives lead to really bad, harmful situations. So I have the hard conversation with them, saying, "It seems like there is a lot going on in your life—now is not the best time for you to go." I then walk with them through those parts of their lives. . . . It is hard to let people know they aren't selected. But in the end, it serves them well. I am gracious and truthful in saying no, and most importantly, it serves our partners well. That's the bigger part of my job [in leading a trip].[6]

Part of serving your partners well means preparing your team for a healthy experience, and that process begins from the moment you present the trip to your congregation. Remember: Patrick and Heather were both describing a trip to the same host. But they painted two very different pictures of what their visit would look like. So foster a different set of expectations, a set of expectations focused on the dignity of the receiving community, God's already existing work, and our long-term role of learning about and humbly engaging in that work.

TAKEAWAYS

- Be sure you have the right leaders to shepherd the members throughout the learning and visit process. Take a moment to think through who from your church might be a good fit.

- Whether through images, announcements, or brochures, be consistent in describing the visit as merely one part of a much larger process of engagement.

- Decide how you will recruit and screen potential participants appropriately, as well as how you will lovingly say no.

.

CHAPTER 8

POSTURE FORMATION AS DISCIPLESHIP

TRAINING THE TEAM

When we first implemented the training, we thought, "Who is going to do that?" But we took a risk and did it anyway. If we truly believe this partnership and work is important, then it is worth the investment. ... If a participant doesn't follow through with the pre-trip prep, we simply tell them that they need to go when they have the time to devote themselves more fully to the long-term process of learning and preparation.[1]

Jason coordinates short-term trips at his church, Cornerstone Community Fellowship, in conjunction with a coalition of churches in his community. As part of that process, Jason and his fellow leaders have developed a required pre-trip training process for participants. But the training consists of more than just three or four meetings to talk about safety precautions, coordinating trips to the airport, and VBS program content. It consists of months of intensive discipleship, cultural and language study, and team building.

CCF's example is a reminder of a sobering truth: if short-term trips truly have an important role in missions and poverty alleviation, and if we, as comparatively affluent believers, are willing to spend thousands of dollars on them, *then we have a heavy responsibility to prepare for those opportunities well, stewarding them to God's glory and the edification of His people.*

NOT AN OPTION

As a leader, you must decide exactly what training will be required, what it will include, and how you will enforce participation in that training. Pre- and post-trip learning is not an optional feature that can be tacked on before a visit. It is an essential part of going to learn, encourage, and engage with your brothers and sisters over time. The process must begin at home, and it is a crucial part of making trips worth it.

Again, it is helpful to remember Brian Howell's observations about the role that expectations play in determining how participants process a trip. Pre-trip training is an opportunity to rehearse a healthy trip narrative focused on learning, fellowship, and long-term engagement.

On a practical level, *Helping Without Hurting in Short-Term Missions: Participant's Guide* canvases the core elements of training, including topics like:

- How a healthier trip model differs from the current STM model, and why

- The relational—not just material—nature of poverty

- Principles of effective poverty alleviation and how to avoid doing harm on a short-term trip. These include:

  —The difference between relief, rehabilitation, and development

  —Asset- vs. needs-based approaches

  —The importance of participation by the materially poor in their own positive change

- How to interact with low-income people in a way that affirms their dignity and seeks to learn from them

• An understanding of cultural differences and why cross-cultural fellowship is important

It is important that you understand these principles well, meaning you will have to review chapters 2–6. You will also have to supplement the *Participant's Guide* with your own resources and country-specific research. If you are going through an intermediary organization, it should provide specific training resources for you to utilize. If not, you will need to invest time aggregating and preparing resources for your team, covering such additional learning elements as:

• Understanding the existing work of ministries and organizations in the community

• Cultural training specific to the receiving community

• The historical, political, economic, and spiritual context of the receiving community

EXPLORING THE CONTEXT

Truly understanding the lives and ministries of your brothers and sisters cannot happen if you detach them from their context. Part of pre-trip preparation should include learning about the physical, cultural, historical, social, and spiritual context of the region. For international trips, consider browsing websites such as the Central Intelligence Agency's *World Factbook* and the BBC's *Country Profiles* database for very general information.[2] Resources like Jason Mandryk's *Operation World* specifically provide context about the church in various countries.[3] For trips within the US, consider again referencing C. E. Elliott's research in "Cross-Cultural Communication Styles," which examines cultural norms and communication patterns among different US groups and communities.[4] Also, revisit George Henderson's *Our Souls to Keep*, particularly chapter 3, for excellent information about European-Americans interacting with African-American individuals and communities.[5] While these resources are not comprehensive, they are a place to start in your own learning.

Resource module B of the *Helping Without Hurting in Short-Term Missions: Participant's Guide* also contains very brief descriptions of the cultural norms discussed in chapter 4 of this guide. While you will need to elaborate on the descriptions in module B when training your team, it should serve as a concise reference tool in the process of cultural training.

Through your research, compile information that addresses community-specific questions like the following:

- What are the religious, linguistic, ethnic, and socioeconomic demographics?

- What are the primary natural resources or industries that drive the economy?

- What are some of the historical and systemic causes of poverty? For example, consider economic or political policies, the collapse of particular industries, natural disasters, wars, ethnic oppression and exploitation, failed educational systems, etc.

- Who are the current political leaders of the city and/or country you will be visiting?

- What is the history of the church in the area? Are Christians persecuted or marginalized? If so, how?

- How do the region's cultural norms differ from your own? What specific gestures or behaviors might you need to avoid?

Involve participants in this process. For example, request that they come to a meeting with a current events article about the area you will be visiting, and discuss what they find. Also, if possible, let community leaders begin to speak for themselves in pre-trip learning. Video chat a staff member or pastor from the receiving community in to your meetings, and have them share about their history, culture, and day-to-day lives. If a member of your own community has lived in or visited the receiving community before, ask him or her to share their experiences. This learning process will continue on the field, but starting it during preparation helps cement the idea that learning is a legitimate goal for the trip.

Furthermore, think through whether there are particular areas of training that may be important, given the context and the experiences of the people with whom you will be interacting. For example, Mark, a missions pastor at Hope Community Church, leads teams of adults who interact with vulnerable women and children in East Africa. He shares, "We want the team to understand why some of the children seem to attach so quickly and the complexity of interacting with them. So we bring in people who work with children with detachment disorders to talk to the team before going."[6] By engaging in this type of specific training, Hope's teams are better prepared to appropriately learn from and encourage the people they encounter, while also guarding against inadvertently harming them.

Finally, on a very practical note, do not forget to cover simple language training if you are traveling overseas or to bilingual communities. Clearly participants will not become even conversationally competent in another language in the space of a few months, and translators will still be essential. But that is not the point. Rather, knowing and attempting to use even a few basic phrases communicates humility as you enter a community. It is a way of recognizing that you are guests in your brothers and sisters' worlds, and that you do not simply expect them to culturally revolve around you. In most cases, members of the receiving community will greatly appreciate the effort.

APPLYING THE PRINCIPLES OF POVERTY ALLEVIATION

Based on their previous experiences, some team members will view the trip as an opportunity to contribute to poverty alleviation. The way that you present the trip and structure the application process will introduce them to the alternative framework of learning, fellowship, encouragement, and long-term engagement. Part of pre-trip training has to involve unpacking the temptation of attempting to directly engage in poverty alleviation during the visit. Rather than using abstract examples, situate your discussion in terms of the specific community you will be visiting.

Go through specific scenarios that team members may encounter on the field, and explain appropriate responses in light of the principles of poverty alleviation and the community's context. Consider the following examples, contextualizing them for your specific situation:

- Your team is supporting a ministry working on a reservation in the Pacific Northwest. A woman asks you to pay a bill for her family of four. In that moment, what do you do? It is tempting to provide the money when you see the poverty around you. But what should you do instead, and why? What church and community leaders would be best equipped to handle the situation, instead of you or a team member giving the money? What cultural and social dynamics may be in play due to the history of the reservation system in the United States? How would giving her the money deepen elements of her poverty?

- You are part of a medical team going to work in a community clinic in Ecuador. The clinic charges patients for its services. Upon arriving and seeing the material poverty around them, several team members want to provide the medical care for free—after all, they are there to serve. But from an economic perspective, how would providing free service impact the clinic down the road? What happens when all of the community members come to get free service, the clinic's supplies are consumed without any reimbursement, and the clinic has nearly zero paying customers for the next month? And what message would it communicate to the patients about their ability to steward their resources and take care of their families? How would providing free services actually deepen elements of the community's poverty?[7]

- Your team is traveling to Haiti, where a local community has initiated and designed a school construction project. As part of your trip, the local community development ministry has offered for your team to assist them in building part of a school, working alongside the community members. When you arrive, the project is behind schedule and none of the community members are present to work on the building. It is just your team and a few of your local contacts. What do you do? Do you work on the project anyway? What would doing so communicate to local people about their ownership of and participation in the project down the road? How would doing work without the community shape your team's perceptions of the local people? How would doing the work undermine the long-term process of poverty alleviation?

Contextualizing and discussing these types of specific, applied examples will help team members to better understand the principles of poverty alleviation, shifting the conversation out of the theoretical realm. But on a deeper level, these conversations also rehearse appropriate responses to the types of situations and emotions the team may face, preventing the team from doing harm during the trip.

MONEY MATTERS

Fundraising, with its support letters and group activities like bake sales and carwashes, seems like a logistical process that is free from any deeper framework implications. In reality, fundraising is an incredible opportunity for team members to practice articulating an alternative vision of what their visit should and will be.

Consider the process of creating a support letter.[8] Besides the logistical information of location, date, and cost, support letters should include the following elements:

- A clear statement of purpose (learning, fellowshiping, encouraging, and engaging with the body of Christ)

- A clear statement of what the trip is not (doing things *for* people or alleviating their poverty in two weeks)

- A brief description of what God is already doing in the receiving community, including an introduction to the work local leaders and organizations are doing

- An explanation of the pre- and post-trip training commitments for team members

- A brief, realistic description of how participants will be spending their time while on the ground

- A statement of the personal financial contribution made and the reason for that investment (without dollar amount)

- An honest description of what the return on investment will be for donors, namely that it will be one step in a process of learning and long-term engagement

- Specific prayer requests, not just for the participants or for the trip, but for the work of the local leaders and organizations you will be visiting

For your reference, resource module A in the *Participant's Guide* includes a sample fundraising letter illustrating these elements.

In the midst of compiling resources, exploring the complexity of poverty alleviation, and casting a different vision for what a short-term trip can be, do not lose sight of the big picture: *this is actually a process of discipleship.* In Jason's words, the extensive pre-trip learning "isn't simply a matter of training. It is a process of formation. . . .We have to prepare *whole people* to go, and to go in the appropriate posture. . . . Ultimately, the goal is for team members to recognize the image of God in each other and in the youth we will be interacting with."[9]

That's an outcome far more transformative and beautiful than any project or task, and it begins before you even step foot on the field.

TAKEAWAYS

- Read through units 1–5 of the *Participant's Guide* and watch the corresponding videos to become familiar with the content.

- Determine what elements you will need to include in pre-field training beyond what is provided in the *Participant's Guide*.

• As needed, recruit people to help you gather information and research for these additional training elements.

• Establish attendance and participation policies for pre-trip training. Decide how you will go about removing someone from the team if they do not attend and participate in these meetings.

CHAPTER 9

THE FIELD AND BEYOND

FROM EXPERIENCE
TO CHANGE

So often, team members would say things like, "If only I knew the language . . ." I would ask them, "What would you do if you *did* know the language?" They would respond, "Well, I would talk to the people I am meeting." My answer was always the same: "You are going back to a place where you *do* know the language. You can be an effective minister for the Lord Jesus Christ there."[1]

Michael and his family spent years ministering in a Majority World country, during which time they hosted over 130 short-term teams. He has seen firsthand the powerful role that short-term trips can have when embedded in a long-term process of change and engagement. His wife, Shelley, describes her perspective on what elements of the field experience lead to transformation: "Lasting transformation happens when participants have multiple opportunities to engage with the local people in meaningful ways."[2]

However, your team will only be on the field for a matter of days. What happens when you return heavily influences whether participants' experiences and interactions will translate into long-term personal and behavioral change. The fact that on-field and post-trip learning are both touched on only briefly in this chapter does not mean that they are unimportant. Rather, this chapter is brief because the *Participant's Guide* covers much of the during- and post-trip material.

WALKING INTENTIONALLY

Whether traveling to a city two hundred miles away or a country on the other half of the world, seeing poverty up close and working through cultural differences is often disorienting. Navigating daily interactions requires keeping the end goals—learning, fellowship, encouragement, and long-term engagement—in mind, and being acutely aware of the potential for unintended harm to the receiving community.

On a practical level, it is important to have an introductory meeting once arriving on the ground, orienting the team to the location, facilities, and other logistics. In addition, formally introduce team members to the local church or organization leaders with whom you will be interacting, allowing those leaders time to explain in person what they do and what God is doing through them.

Sometime during the first day, also skim unit 6 of the *Participant's Guide* as a team. Encourage team members to keep these prompts in mind during the day and to allot personal time in the evening for them to jot down their thoughts. Throughout the trip, have debriefing meetings at least every two to three days, allowing participants to share their thoughts and observations together. Because you presented the trip as a learning opportunity and completed pre-trip training, the team members should be willing to engage in these types of conversations. The final pages of unit 6 are designed for the last evening of the trip. Use these prompts to help participants to begin reflecting on their time and to begin thinking through how they will steward the experience.

However, do not create an environment in any of the on-field meetings that pressures participants to stretch their experiences into something profound. Participants will process the trip in different ways. The goal of on-field journaling is to observe and record experiences. The bulk of deeper reflection will occur when you have returned home. Your goal as a leader is to provide space and guidance as participants wrestle with their experiences *over time*, not to foster an environment that burdens team members to find immediate meaning each night at the expense of reflective, nuanced thinking.

NAVIGATING POVERTY

When participants see material poverty around them, they will be tempted to slip back into "doing" and "fixing" mode, no longer focusing on the gifts and assets that God has placed in the community. Further, some team members will struggle with the chasm in material condition between their lives and the members of the receiving community. Some participants will feel guilty about their relative wealth. Richard Slimbach, a professor at Azusa Pacific University and expert in global studies, describes another common reaction. Being confronted with extreme wealth disparities often leads people to simply feel grateful that they were "lucky" enough to avoid poverty. But in his words:

> Interpreting complex situations through this kind of "lotto logic" evades any serious analysis of the geographic conditions, historical relations, and real abuses . . . that explain the disparities they observe. It can also allow an ignited sense of social responsibility to be extinguished by a naïve faith in the justice of fate. . . . The challenge for STM leaders is to help move participant thinking beyond "luck explanations" of inequality by exploring *why* these conditions exist and *how* their lives intersect with the lives of residents.[3]

The purpose of a visit is not to feel guilty about having material resources or to be thankful that you "lucked out." As your team encounters poverty on the field, encourage them to move past emotional reactions to the realm of observing and questioning their assumptions. Digging deeper in to poverty—and a healthy response to it—will continue to be a significant theme as you return home.

BEING A BLESSING

Interacting with believers in the receiving community must involve intentionally respecting and encouraging them at all times, being "quick to listen, slow to speak" (James 1:19). Obey the directions and instructions of your hosts, even when it may go against what you had hoped the trip would be. Be flexible, accepting that plans may change at a moment's notice as cars break down, weather does not cooperate, or your hosts' schedules change. And to the best of your ability, be mindful of the cultural norms and customs of the receiving community.

But none of that means that you, as a leader, are passive while on the field. Submitting to local leadership does not mean abdicating responsibility. Encourage team members to refrain from making quick judgments, especially about things that are different from their normal experiences. Your role is to lead by example, to shepherd your team emotionally and spiritually, and to be aware of any potential dangers of inadvertent harm.

On a seemingly mundane note, also be aware of how participants are utilizing social media and photography during the trip. Coming from a culture where seemingly every meal, sunset, and cat is instantly documented online, team members often do not think about the messages they send through pictures and status updates. Unit 5 of the *Participant's Guide* provides specific guidelines for photography and social media use, many of which are based on the principles discussed in chapter 7 of this *Leader's Guide*. If you see participants operating outside of those guidelines, privately chat with them about how they can better respect the receiving community while recording their experiences.

It may sound extreme, but consider prohibiting social media and cellphone use during your time on the field. While safety and communication needs will require contact between leaders and families back home, challenge participants to be *fully present* during this experience. Deeper, more reflective learning will occur without the distraction of describing and live documenting their experience for an online audience.

COMING HOME

Kurt Ver Beek, in his research about the impact of short-term missions, describes factors that seemingly contribute to long-term transformation in trip participants. These elements, which he labels "accountability" and "encouragement," help foster lasting change in team members' hearts and behaviors.[4] How the encouragement and accountability process works will vary from church to church in terms of the specific structure of individual meetings and follow-up. But it may be helpful to think of the process in the following stages.

- **Reflection and Analysis**: Within two weeks after arriving home, gather the team to discuss how returning to their daily lives is going. Spend time looking over and discussing journal entries from unit 6 of the *Participant's Guide*, sharing the things team members saw that intrigued them, confused them, or moved them. Then work through unit 7. As instructed on the last evening of the trip, participants should come to this meeting with their basic thoughts already recorded for this unit. These questions are designed to lead participants to more deeply consider the poverty and cultural differences they observed, as well as reflect on the rich beauty of the body of Christ. Spend as much time as necessary unpacking these questions—it may take more than one session to work through them.

- **Set and Share Goals:** Unit 8 of the *Participant's Guide* focuses on what it looks like to tangibly engage with the body of Christ, to support the brothers and sisters you interacted with during your trip, and to continue the process of learning and engagement in your own community. Aim to begin this unit no later than three weeks after returning. As participants determine how they wish to move forward, they should create written SMART goals (Specific, Measurable, Area-specific, Realistic, and Time-bound). The goal-setting process may span two sessions in order to flesh out the goals and accountability summaries. Have participants share these goals and accountability steps with one another and their supporters. If teams typically present a report to your church as a whole, have the team share their experiences, what they learned, *and* these goals.

- **Report Back to Supporters:** Once participants have reflected on their experiences and set SMART goals, walk with them as they create a follow-up letter to their supporters. Participants have a responsibility to share with their supporters how they are moving forward. In addition, just as a fundraising letter is an opportunity to rehearse a healthy set of expectations about what a short-term trip should be, the follow-up letter is an opportunity for participants to rehearse and commit to being a good steward of the experience.

- **Maintain Accountability:** The process is not over when you reach the end of unit 8. Continue meeting on a monthly or bimonthly basis, holding each other accountable for the goals set in unit 8. The questions outlined in "Checking In" at the end of unit 8 are potential prompts for these meetings. Encourage one another, fellowship together, and pray for the community you visited. Discuss how you are applying and embodying in your own community the things you learned. Roughly six months after the trip, watch the video for unit 8 again at one of your meetings. How have you stewarded the experience of the trip? Have you followed through on the goals you set, making the financial resources invested in the trip worth it? How has the way you engage with and pray for your own community changed? Has the way you view material poverty and poverty alleviation changed? If so, how? If not, why not? How are you coming to a deeper understanding of your own poverty—i.e., your own brokenness?

The ability to travel hundreds, or even thousands, of miles to interact with our brothers and sisters is a remarkable gift. What we do with that gift matters. So let's be sensitive to our brothers and sisters as we plan a trip and enter their communities, ensuring that we do not accidentally harm them. And let's manage the experience well, ensuring that we are making the thousands of dollars we spend on these trips—and the hours our hosts pour in to them—count for lasting change in our own neighborhoods, our own hearts, and our brothers and sisters' lives around the world.

TAKEAWAYS

- Read through units 6–8 of the *Participant's Guide* and watch the last video segment to be familiar with the content.

- Be sure the field visit schedule has time for members to complete unit 6 exercises well.

- Determine the number of post-field meetings that will be required and the schedule for those meetings.

FINAL ENCOURAGEMENT: RESPOND, DON'T OVERREACT

Something interesting happened after the publication of *When Helping Hurts*. By God's grace, thousands of people began applying the principles described in the book, engaging in more effective poverty alleviation approaches in their communities and around the world. But something else happened as well. Some churches, leaders, and ministries felt a bit paralyzed after reading the book. They put the book down, realizing that they may have been doing inadvertent harm, but they were unsure of how to apply the principles moving forward. So some stopped trying to help poor people altogether.

That was never our intent. Our passion is for churches, ministries, and individual Christians to substantially increase their efforts to help poor people. We just want all of us to do so more effectively.

Similarly, in this guide we have outlined some stark realities about STMs as they are currently practiced. But we believe there is a way forward. And the way forward isn't in *reacting* to these ideas emotionally, withdrawing from poverty alleviation and missions, and swinging from one extreme to another. Nor do we want you to become fearful and paralyzed. The way forward is in *responding*, prayerfully reflecting on where and how God is asking you to change, and then applying those realizations to your actions. Responding likely means adapting how you do short-term trips, or maybe even pausing your short-term program and rebuilding it from the ground up. And yes, it may mean substantially reducing your short-term trip budget and reallocating these funds to approaches and ministries that will have a more positive and deeper impact on the lives of materially poor people. Hence, both this guide and *When Helping Hurts* are about engaging more deeply and giving even more generously to missions and poverty alleviation than ever before. The point is just to engage and to give differently.

One last reminder: as stated in chapter 2, a portion of short-term trip participant fees sometimes goes to support the ministry, church, or organization you are going through or visiting. *In these scenarios, if you cancel your trip without increasing your engagement with and giving to them, you may be harming the work they are doing.* There may be times when you do have to adjust where you give in order to steward your resources well, particularly in regard to short-term trips. There may be times that you need to pull back from work that you realize is actually creating dependency. But be humble and careful as you make those decisions. We don't want you to accidentally withdraw support from effective ministry and poverty alleviation work.

Reforming short-term trips is a process. The ministry leaders that we have talked to, including those who have been operating from a healthier trip approach for years, have said one common thing: "It is messy. We are still trying to figure it out, but it's so worth it." So be encouraged. You aren't alone in attempting to shift the inertia of your church. You aren't alone in trying to move toward healthier short-term trips. You aren't alone in making difficult, sometimes unpopular, decisions.

And most important, you aren't alone in longing for glimpses of Christ's ultimate restoration to invade the brokenness of this world and for the good news of the gospel to be proclaimed and demonstrated among people who are poor. Brothers and sisters in your own community and across the globe stand with you in that longing, a longing that is itself the Spirit working in and through you.

You see, ultimately *this is God's work, not ours.* He is the one who is restoring all things. The success or failure of His cosmic plan is not contingent on whether or not we perfectly engage in poverty alleviation. In fact, we never will do it perfectly. *The joy is that God does not require perfection from us; rather, He asks us to be faithful servants who learn from our mistakes.* When we let fear of doing it wrong lead us into paralysis, we are letting our god-complexes get in the way. We are acting as though our efforts are the bottom line, rather than the God who can use our humble—albeit imperfect—service for His glory and kingdom.

So get moving. Make hard decisions in prayer, love, humility, and discernment. Support and engage with the work God is doing in even more generous and intentional ways. And rejoice that one day He will complete the work He has started.

SUGGESTED RESOURCES

Deeper Learning about STMs

- "Standards of Excellence in Short-Term Mission"—A helpful outline of best practices in STMs. See www.soe.org.

- David Livermore, *Serving with Eyes Wide Open: Doing Short-Term Missions with Cultural Intelligence*—An excellent story-filled resource exploring what healthy trips look like, particularly cross-cultural visits.

- Brian M. Howell, *Short-Term Mission: An Ethnography of Christian Travel Narrative and Experience*—A more academic look at the origins and current practice of STMs.

Partnerships

- Coalition on the Support of Indigenous Ministries (COSIM): A network of people and organizations dedicated to healthy cross-cultural partnerships. See www.cosim.info.

- Daniel Rickett. *Making Your Partnership Work: A Guide for Ministry Leaders* and *Building Strategic Relationships: A Practical Guide for Partnering with Non-Western Missions*—These books and Rickett's website, www.danielrickett.com, provide excellent counsel on healthy partnerships.

- *The Beauty of Partnership Study Guide,* edited by Werner Mischke and created by Mission ONE—A six-week course on navigating cross-cultural partnerships. See http://beautyofpartnership.org/.

Cultural Differences and Cross-Cultural Engagement

- Duane Elmer, *Cross Cultural Conflict: Building Relationships for Effective Ministry* and *Cross-Cultural Servanthood: Serving the World in Christlike Humility*—These provide excellent perspective on the complexity of culture, particularly within the body of Christ.

- George Henderson, *Our Souls to Keep: Black/White Relations in America*—Helpful perspective for European-American teams entering African-American contexts.

- David Livermore, *Serving with Eyes Wide Open*—Again, excellent reflection on the nuances of cultural differences in the context of STMs.

- David Maranz, *African Friends and Money Matters: Observations from Africa*—Crucial perspective for anyone entering long-term partnerships in an African context.

- Craig Storti, *Figuring Foreigners Out: A Practical Guide*—Further context and information about cultural norms and differences.

NOTES

Introduction—The Need for This Guide

1. To browse the Standards in brief or full-length form, visit "The 7 Standards," Standards of Excellence in Short-Term Mission, accessed March 18, 2014, http://www.soe.org/explore/the-7-standards/.

Chapter 1—Mission Accomplished?

1. Data in this paragraph are from Roger Peterson, plenary address at Short-Term Missions Long-Term Impact?, a conference cosponsored by Interdenominational Foreign Missions Association and the Evangelical Missiological Society, September 28, 2007, Minneapolis, MN.

2. Gathering comprehensive data on the scale of a movement as diverse as STMs is challenging, and thus different approaches yield slightly different results. Some research has found that the growth rate of STMs may be slowing. See A. Scott Moreau, "A Current Snapshot of North American Protestant Missions," *International Bulletin of Missionary Research* 35, no. 1 (January 2011): 12. However, researchers seem united in recognizing the prevalence, importance, and popularity of STMs in the life of US churches, and there is no evidence to suggest the movement will dissipate any time soon.

3. Robert J. Priest, "Short-Term Missions as a New Paradigm," in *Mission After Christendom: Emergent Themes in Contemporary Mission*, ed. Ogbu U. Kalu, Peter Vethanayagamony, and Edmund Kee-Fook Chia (Louisville, KY: Westminster John Knox Press, 2010), 86.

4. Robert Wuthnow, *Boundless Faith: The Global Outreach of American Churches* (Berkeley, CA: University of California Press, 2009), 171.

5. The following section draws on Brian M. Howell, *Short-Term Mission: An Ethnography of Christian Travel Narrative and Experience* (Downers Grove, IL: InterVarsity Press, 2012), particularly chapters 3, 4, and 5.

6. Ibid., 97.

7. A. Scott Moreau, "Short-Term Missions in the Context of Missions, Inc.," in *Effective Engagement in Short-Term Missions: Doing it Right!*, ed. Robert J. Priest (Pasadena, CA: William Carey Library, 2008), 16.

8. Kurt Alan Ver Beek, "Lessons from the Sapling: Review of the Quantitative Research on Short-Term Missions," in *Effective Engagement in Short-Term Missions: Doing it Right!*, 479–80.

9. Moreau, "Short-Term Missions in the Context of Missions, Inc.," 15, shows no increase in long-term missionary numbers as a result of STMs as of 2005 data. However, data from 2008 show an increase in long-term missionaries from the agencies surveyed. See Moreau, "A Current Snapshot of North

American Protestant Missions," 12. Whether this 2008 data are indicative of a trend, and if so, whether the increase is related to STM participation, is a subject for further research.

10. For further reflection about the relative lack of ongoing transformation in participants of STMs as they are currently practiced, see Rolando W. Cuellar, "Short-Term Missions Are Bigger Than You Think: Missiological Implications for the Glocal Church," in *Effective Engagement in Short-Term Missions: Doing it Right!*, 281–85.

11. LiErin Probasco, "Giving Time, Not Money: Long-term Impacts of Short-term Mission Trips," *Missiology: An International Review* 41, no. 2 (2013): 216, 219.

12. Ibid., 220.

13. See Ver Beek, "Lessons from the Sapling," in *Effective Engagement in Short-Term Missions: Doing it Right!*, 477–79; David A. Livermore, *Serving with Eyes Wide Open: Doing Short-Term Missions with Cultural Intelligence* (Grand Rapids, MI: Baker Publishing Group, 2006), 55–57.

Chapter 2—"Do Unto Others"

1. Robert J. Priest and Joseph Paul Priest, "'They see everything and understand nothing': Short-Term Mission and Service Learning," *Missiology* 36, no. 1 (January 2008): 57.

2. Robert Wuthnow and Stephen Offutt, "Transnational Religious Connections," *Sociology of Religion* 69, no. 2 (2008): 218.

3. Robert Wuthnow, *Boundless Faith: The Global Outreach of American Churches* (Berkeley: University of California Press, 2009), 180.

4. Jo Ann Van Engen, "The Cost of Short-Term Missions," *The Other Side* 36 (January-February 2000): 20.

5. Kurt Alan Ver Beek, "Lessons from the Sapling," in *Effective Engagement in Short-Term Missions: Doing it Right!*, ed. Robert J. Priest (Pasadena, CA: William Carey Library, 2008), 477.

6. "How Sponsorship Works and Financial Integrity," Gospel for Asia, accessed January 23, 2014, http://www.gfa.org/sponsor/sponsor-info/.

7. Dennis Horton, Sarah Caldwell, Rachel Calhoun, Josh Flores, Chris Gerac, and Gabrielle Leonard, "Short-Term Mission Trips: What the Long-Term Mission Personnel Really Think about Them," *The Year 2013 Annual Proceedings of the ASSR*, ed. Jon K. Loessin and Scott Stripling (2013): 71.

8. A. Scott Moreau, "Short-Term Missions in the Context of Missions, Inc.," in *Effective Engagement in Short-Term Missions: Doing it Right!*, 16.

9. James Lai, quoted in Enoch Wan and Geoffrey Hartt, "Complementary Aspects of Short-Term Missions and Long-Term Missions: Case Studies for a

Win-Win Situation," in *Effective Engagement in Short-Term Missions: Doing it Right!*, 84–85.

10. This is a modification of the definition of paternalism found in Roland Bunch, *Two Ears of Corn: A Guide to People-Centered Agricultural Improvement* (Oklahoma City, OK: World Neighbors, 1982).

11. Local job opportunities being totally dependent on foreign funding is clearly problematic. However, there is room for outside money to be mobilized alongside community-initiated projects, contributing to the economic development of an area and supporting job opportunities on projects that will lead to long-term community benefit. As Daniel Rickett argues in *Making Your Partnership Work: A Guide for Ministry Leaders* (Enumclaw, WA: WinePress Publishing, 2002), there is such a thing as healthy interdependence in economic development—both parties should have space to use their God-given gifts in concert.

12. Dennis Horton et al., "Short-Term Mission Trips," 75. Horton's research also provides a helpful explanation of why construction projects are so popular during STMs. He highlights the potentially problematic need for teams to "do" something, while also recognizing the potential benefits of participants and community members working together, if the project is designed appropriately.

13. David A. Livermore, *Serving with Eyes Wide Open: Doing Short-Term Missions with Cultural Intelligence* (Grand Rapids, MI: Baker Publishing Group, 2006), 90–91.

14. James Ward, interview by Katie Casselberry and Andy Jones, Atlanta, GA, August 23, 2013.

15. Anonymous, "Short-Term Missions Can Create a Long-Term Mess," *Mandate*, Chalmers Center for Economic Development, 2007, no. 3, available at www.chalmers.org.

16. Livermore, *Serving with Eyes Wide Open*, 106.

Chapter 3—Presence or Projects

1. David A. Livermore, *Serving with Eyes Wide Open: Doing Short-Term Missions with Cultural Intelligence* (Grand Rapids, MI: Baker Publishing Group, 2006), 95–96.

2. Sam Moore, interview by Katie Casselberry, Lookout Mountain, GA, January 15, 2013.

3. "Shelley," interview by Katie Casselberry, March 11, 2014.

4. Kyeong Sook Park, "Researching Short-Term Missions and Paternalism," in *Effective Engagement in Short-Term Missions: Doing it Right!*, ed. Robert J. Priest (Pasadena, CA: William Carey Library, 2008), 516, 524–25.

5. Marco Perez, interview by Katie Casselberry, Lookout Mountain, GA, January 15, 2013.

6. Ibid.

7. "Jason," interview by Katie Casselberry, October 30, 2013.

8. Kurt Kandler, interview by Katie Casselberry and Andy Jones, Atlanta, GA, August 23, 2013.

9. These ideas are not necessarily new. Multiple people and organizations have called for these types of principles to inform short-term trips. See, for example, "The Standards of Excellence in Short-Term Missions;" Howell, *Short-Term Mission*; Ver Beek, "Lessons from the Sapling;" Miriam Adeney, "The Myth of the Blank Slate: A Check List for Short-Term Missions," in *Effective Engagement in Short-Term Missions: Doing it Right!*; Edwin Zehner, "On the Rhetoric of Short-Term Missions Appeals, with Some Practical Suggestions for Team Leaders," in *Effective Engagement in Short-Term Missions: Doing it Right!*.

10. Dennis Horton, Sarah Caldwell, Rachel Calhoun, Josh Flores, Chris Gerac, and Gabrielle Leonard, "Short-Term Mission Trips: What the Long-Term Mission Personnel Really Think about Them," *The Year 2013 Annual Proceedings of the ASSR*, ed. Jon K. Loessin and Scott Stripling (2013): 77.

11. Brian M. Howell, *Short-Term Mission: An Ethnography of Christian Travel Narrative and Experience* (Downers Grove, IL: InterVarsity Press, 2012), 221, 233.

Chapter 4—Preparing for Complexity

1. See David E. Maranz, *African Friends and Money Matters* (Dallas, TX: SIL International, 2001).

2. Duane H. Elmer, *Cross-Cultural Conflict: Building Relationships for Effective Ministry* (Downers Grove, IL: InverVarsity Press, 1993), 52.

3. A summary and adaptation of Elliott's work is available in Candia Elliott, R. Jerry Adams, and Suganya Sockalingham, "Communication Patterns and Assumptions of Differing Cultural Groups in the United States," in *Toolkit for Cross-Cultural Collaboration* (2010), accessed April 17, 2014, http://www.awesomelibrary.org/multiculturaltoolkit-patterns.html.

4. George Henderson, *Our Souls to Keep: Black/White Relations in America* (Yarmouth, ME: Intercultural Press, Inc., 1999).

5. Meera Komarraju and Kevin O. Cokley, "Horizontal and Vertical Dimensions of Individualism-Collectivism," *Cultural Diversity and Ethnic Minority Psychology* 14, no. 4 (October 2008): 338.

6. Man Keung Ho, Janice Matthews Rasheed, and Mikal N. Rasheed, *Family Therapy with Ethnic Minorities*, 2nd ed. (Thousand Oaks, CA: Sage Publications, 2004), 285; Garrett McAuliffe, *Culturally Alert Counseling: A Comprehensive Introduction* (Thousand Oaks, CA: Sage Publications, 2008), 158.

7. Komarraju and Cokley, "Horizontal and Vertical Dimensions of Individualism-Collectivism," 338; Ho, et al., *Family Therapy with Ethnic Minorities*, 287.

8. Henderson, *Our Souls to Keep*, 52–53.

9. Duane Elmer, *Cross-Cultural Servanthood: Serving the World in Christlike Humility* (Downers Grove, IL: InterVarsity Press, 2006).

Chapter 5—Dancing Well

1. Miriam Adeney, "The Myth of the Blank Slate," in *Effective Engagement in Short-Term Missions: Doing it Right!*, ed. Robert J. Priest (Pasadena, CA: William Carey Library, 2008), 132.

2. Daniel Rickett, *Making Your Partnership Work*; Daniel Rickett, *Building Strategic Relationships: A Practical Guide to Partnering with Non-Western Missions*, 3rd ed. (Minneapolis, MN: STEM Press, 2008).

3. Werner Mischke, ed., *The Beauty of Partnership Study Guide* (Scottsdale, AZ: Mission ONE, 2010).

4. "Ryan," interview by Katie Casselberry, December 5, 2013.

5. "Jason," interview.

Chapter 6—Overcoming Inertia

1. Roland Bunch, *Two Ears of Corn: A Guide to People-Centered Agricultural Improvement* (Oklahoma City, OK: World Neighbors, 1982), 21–36.

2. Miriam Adeney, "The Myth of the Blank Slate," in *Effective Engagement in Short-Term Missions: Doing it Right!*, ed. Robert J. Priest (Pasadena, CA: William Carey Library, 2008), 138.

3. This section draws on suggestions about connecting congregations to the work of long-term missions provided by Adeney, "The Myth of the Blank Slate," 138–44.

4. David A. Livermore, *Serving with Eyes Wide Open: Doing Short-Term Missions with Cultural Intelligence* (Grand Rapids, MI: Baker Publishing Group, 2006), 94.

Chapter 7—Some Assembly Required

1. Brian M. Howell, *Short-Term Mission: An Ethnography of Christian Travel Narrative and Experience* (Downers Grove, IL: InterVarsity Press, 2012), 24, 129. This chapter is heavily influenced by Howell's observations and insights.

2. This section draws on Edwin Zehner, "On the Rhetoric of Short-Term Missions Appeals," in *Effective Engagement in Short-Term Missions: Doing it Right!*. ed. Robert J. Priest (Pasadena, CA: William Carey Library, 2008), 198–99.

3. Ward, interview.

4. "Ryan," interview.

5. Gregg Burgess, interview by Katie Casselberry, Lookout Mountain, GA, January 15, 2013.

6. "Mark," interview by Katie Casselberry, November 7, 2013.

Chapter 8—Posture Formation as Discipleship

1. "Jason," interview.

2. See *"The World Factbook,"* Central Intelligence Agency, https://www.cia.gov/library/publications/the-world-factbook/. *"Country Profiles,"* The BBC, http://news.bbc.co.uk/2/hi/country_profiles/.

3. Jason Mandryk, *Operation World: The Definitive Prayer Guide to Every Nation* (Downers Grove, IL: InterVarsity Press, 2010).

4. Candia Elliott in Elliott, Adams, and Sockalingham, "Communication Patterns and Assumptions of Differing Cultural Groups in the United States," in *Toolkit for Cross-Cultural Collaboration* (2010), accessed April 17, 2014, http://www.awesomelibrary.org/multiculturaltoolkit-patterns.html.

5. George Henderson, *Our Souls to Keep: Black/White Relations in America* (Yarmouth, ME: Intercultural Press, Inc., 1999).

6. "Mark," interview.

7. Based on a story from Kurt Kandler interview.

8. Brian M. Howell, *Short-Term Mission: An Ethnography of Christian Travel Narrative and Experience* (Downers Grove, IL: InterVarsity Press, 2012), 133–38, provides an excellent discussion of how the traditional STM framework is often embodied and rehearsed in the fundraising process.

9. "Jason," interview.

Chapter 9—The Field and Beyond

1. "Michael," interview by Katie Casselberry, March 11, 2014.

2. "Shelley," interview.

3. Richard Slimbach, "The Mindful Missioner," in *Effective Engagement in Short-Term Missions: Doing it Right!*, ed. Robert J. Priest (Pasadena, CA: William Carey Library, 2008), 163–164.

4. Kurt Alan Ver Beek, "Lessons from the Sapling," in *Effective Engagement in Short-Term Missions: Doing it Right!*, ed. Robert J. Priest (Pasadena, CA: William Carey Library, 2008), 494.

PARTICIPANT'S GUIDE WITH SCRIPTING

CONTENTS

INTRODUCTION:
HOW TO USE THIS GUIDE

Over the past two decades, there has been an enormous increase in comparatively affluent churches' efforts to help the poor. One way churches are seeking to engage in poverty alleviation is through short-term missions (STMs.) After writing *When Helping Hurts*, countless church and ministry leaders approached us for further resources to design and shepherd short-term teams effectively. *Helping Without Hurting in Short-Term Missions* is designed to meet that request in a practical way.

The *Participant's Guide* is available as a standalone product.

ACCESSING THE VIDEO UNITS

Units 1–5 and unit 8 are built around fifiteen- to twenty-minute videos, which can be accessed by following the link or QR code printed in each unit. When prompted, set up an account with your information and the code printed in the unit. The videos are also available to RightNow Media account holders (www.rightnowmedia.org).

UNIT STRUCTURE

With the exception of unit 6, which is an on-field journaling and reflection unit, each unit will take about ninety minutes to complete. Here is a breakdown of the different sections of the lessons, as well as rough time estimates for each:

OPEN (10 minutes): This section includes preliminary questions and an introductory paragraph. Discussing the preliminary questions as a group is a vital part of mentally and spiritually preparing for the rest of the unit.

WATCH (20 minutes): Group members should close their books while watching the video so that they can fully listen to and engage with the material.

DISCUSS (40 minutes): These questions are designed to create discussion—they do not necessarily have right or wrong answers. The goal is to foster reflection, understanding, and change in participants' hearts as they consider the purpose of a short-term trip. As such, it is important to give adequate time for discussion. Don't be afraid of a bit of silence, and don't be afraid of asking people to expand on their answers. There is enormous power in having people wrestle with questions and issues together, so long as it is done in a spirit of respect. The scripting in the *Leader's Guide* printing of this material will help you navigate these interactions. If you are using the *Participant's Guide* with teens, be aware that you may want to tweak some of the questions based on your context.

TAKEAWAYS and **CLOSE** (10 minutes): Read this material together as you conclude the session. Ask if anyone has questions. If there is not time to adequately discuss each one, ask the group to contemplate their questions throughout the week.

PRAY (10 minutes): Use this final statement and prayer prompt as a call for reflection and action. Encourage participants to return to this prompt as they pray throughout the week, and then close in prayer together.

In addition to the basic units, the resource modules at the end of this guide provide additional materials on fundraising and cultural norms.

We cannot overemphasize the centrality of prayer in this process. The principles in this guide require that all of us honestly examine our own hearts and actions as we approach STMs. Spend time praying that God would soften your hearts as you begin the long-term process of learning and engagement with His work in the world. But also pray that your group would see, internalize, and celebrate the hope rooted in Christ.

Our brothers and sisters, both in our own communities and around the world, are proclaiming and demonstrating the good news of Christ's power and redemptive sacrifice. The journey you are about to begin is an opportunity to see, support, and move toward long-term engagement in that work. So eagerly anticipate what God will do through this opportunity, and marvel as God makes both the materially poor—and us—more of who He originally intended for us to be.

— Steve Corbett and Brian Fikkert

LEARNING AND ENGAGEMENT AGREEMENT

I, _____, recognize that by joining this learning and engagement journey, I am committing to more than simply visiting another community. I am committing to attend and participate in weeks of preparation, as well as submitting to the authority of my team leader and local hosts. Further, I am committing to stewarding the experience well, making my use of God's resources on this trip count for lasting change in my own life, attitudes, and behaviors. I agree to attend and participate in follow-up meetings with my team, where we will set concrete goals for how we might continue to support God's work of missions and poverty alleviation, encourage one another, and hold each other accountable to pursuing these goals.

Date:

Signature:

Leader's Signature:

UNIT 1

MORE THAN
MEETS THE **EYE**

Discuss these questions before beginning this week's unit.

• What are the first five words or phrases that come to your mind when you think of poverty?

• If you had to describe the purpose of this short-term trip in one sentence, what would it be?

• What are your personal goals for this trip? Two years from now, what are two things in your life and actions that you would like to be different as a result of going on this trip?

MISSION ACCOMPLISHED?

Aubrey sat in the back row of the fifteen-passenger van, awkwardly curled up with her legs on top of her backpack. The rest of the team was sleeping, heads leaning against windows and piles of pillows. Aubrey, though, was staring into the distance, exhausted but unable to sleep. She kept thinking of Michelle, a ten-year-old girl from Chicago she had befriended over the past six days. Images of her adorable grin played on repeat in her mind. Each morning, Aubrey and her fellow team members worked on houses in Michelle's neighborhood, and then ran VBS classes in the afternoon. Last night, Aubrey had to say goodbye. She tearfully gave Michelle a box of candy and school supplies. *It kills me to leave, but I know we both understand Jesus better because I was faithful to come here, sacrificing my time and resources to love her*, Aubrey thought as the van pulled into a filling station.

At first glance, it seems like Aubrey and her team successfully acted on their biblical command to love and serve people who are poor. After all, houses were freshly painted, and the neighborhood children had bracelets representing the gospel story the team had shared. But if Aubrey could spend months, or years, in that neighborhood, she would realize that alleviating poverty isn't that straightforward—her team may have recognized the symptoms of poverty, but there was actually something more happening beneath the surface.

WATCH

Close your books and watch this week's video via the QR code or link below.

 www.helpingwithouthurting.org/stm-videos

Follow the prompts to set up an account or sign back in, utilizing the access code below to view the videos:

Code: COL120

DISCUSS

Initial Reflections

1. What are two or three ideas that struck you in the video? What questions do you have after seeing the video?

MAKING IT COUNT

Consider the following numbers and statistics:

- **2–3 million people:** 2010 estimate of how many people from the United States go on short-term mission trips (STMs) internationally each year[1]

- **20–25 percent:** The likelihood of any given church member going on an international STM sometime in their lifetime as of 2009[2]

- **$1,370–$1,450 per person:** Range of average cost for an international STM[3]

- **$1.6 *billion*:** A conservative estimate of international STM spending per year—that's $1,600,000,000[4]

- **4 million people:** number of the world's extreme poor whose *yearly* income would equal the $1.6 billion spent on international STMs in one year[5]

- **$3,000–$6,000 per year:** the range of *yearly* salary for a community-level relief and development worker in the Majority World—an STM of fifteen people at $1,400 per person would spend $21,000, an amount that could support three to seven staff members for a year

1. Out of the above numbers, what statistics surprise you the most? Why?

These numbers paint a sobering picture. Simply put, we spend a massive amount of money on short-term trips—money that could be used to support people working and ministering in their own communities, people who are already familiar with the context and culture of the community. These people could be used by God to evangelize, disciple, and combat poverty over the long haul.

2. Given this reality, how do you justify using God's money to go on this trip?

   Help participants avoid the extremes of either:

   —*Treating this information too lightly, assuming that their contribution on the trip will be so significant that the visit will automatically be worth it.*

   —*Guilty desperation, doubting whether participating in a visit could ever be a good use of God's money.*

So why go? As we will see throughout these lessons, the purpose of a trip isn't primarily about what you will do or what impact you will have in two weeks. It's about what you can learn, in deep and meaningful ways, and how that learning can translate into long-term engagement in the world of missions and poverty alleviation.

REDEFINING POVERTY

How we define poverty will heavily influence how we respond to and attempt to alleviate that poverty. Take a moment to review the table below of commonly cited causes and responses to poverty:

If We Believe the Primary Cause of Poverty Is . . .	Then We Will Primarily Try to . . .
A Lack of Knowledge	Educate the Poor
Oppression by Powerful People	Work for Social Justice
The Personal Sins of the Poor	Evangelize and Disciple the Poor
A Lack of Material Resources	Give Material Resources to the Poor

1. Look back at your answers to the preliminary questions. Do your answers about poverty tend to emphasize one particular category above?

   —*During the discussion, be sure to emphasize that all of these are factors of and manifestations of poverty.*

   —*Discuss why emphasizing one/some factors and underemphasizing others would be problematic.*

2. Which line(s) of the table above do you think short-term trips most frequently try to address, and how do they typically do it? Why do you think this is the case?

—*Many people will say that short-term trips focus on addressing a lack of material things, emphasizing doing things for or giving things to the materially poor that are tangible.*

—*Why is this the case? Again, this goes back to a material understanding of the world and poverty.*

COMPLEXITY COUNTS

Because God is inherently relational and made humans in His image, humans are wired for relationship, too. When the four relationships are functioning properly, humans experience the fullness of life that God intended—we are being what God created us to be.

THE FOUR FOUNDATIONAL RELATIONSHIPS

Adapted from Bryant L. Myers, *Walking with the Poor: Principles and Practices of Transformational Development* (Maryknoll, NY: Orbis Books, 1999), 27.

But as we discussed in the video, the fall broke these relationships.

THE FOUR BROKEN RELATIONSHIPS

Adapted from Bryant L. Myers, *Walking with the Poor: Principles and Practices of Transformational Development* (Maryknoll, NY: Orbis Books, 1999), 27.

From this framework, poverty isn't only about a lack of material things. While that is an important element of poverty, there are many other crucial factors at work. As a result, poverty—and poverty alleviation—is complex.

POVERTY

"Poverty is the result of relationships that do not work, that are not just, that are not for life, that are not harmonious or enjoyable. Poverty is the absence of shalom in all its meanings."

—**Bryant Myers**, *Walking with the Poor*[6]

Remember: because the fall impacted *everything*, both individual people and systems are broken. The brokenness in the four relationships means social, political, economic, and religious systems are marred by sin. Thus, poverty alleviation also involves transforming those systems. Sometimes people blame choices made by the materially poor for their poverty, arguing that anyone could escape poverty if they wanted to do so. While sinful individual choices can contribute to poverty, poverty is also the result of circumstances outside the control of the materially poor. For example, consider the prevalence of poverty in many US cities. Many neighborhoods bear the marks of centuries of racial discrimination and damaging economic, social, and political policies. What happens when society crams historically oppressed, undereducated, unemployed, and relatively young human beings into high-rise buildings, provides them with inferior education, healthcare, and employment systems, and then establishes financial disincentives for work? Is it really that surprising that we see out-of-wedlock pregnancies, broken families, violent crimes, and drug trafficking? Yes, those choices are still wrong. But they have a context. Both broken systems and broken individual choices contribute to poverty.

Part of the learning process of a short-term trip entails recalibrating our hearts and minds, moving away from easy—but incomplete and unbiblical—assumptions about the materially poor. Learning about and acknowledging the complexity of poverty, particularly in the community you will be visiting, is an essential part of long-term engagement in missions and poverty alleviation.

1. When you interact with the materially poor, do you tend to see their poverty more as a result of their personal actions or circumstances beyond their control?

   —*It is common within many evangelical circles to focus primarily on the personal actions that can contribute to poverty. If the group's tendency is to see personal actions as the root of poverty, your job will be to help them see some of the structural realities that also cause and entrap people in poverty.*

   —*Utilize some specific information about the historical and social context of the community you will be visiting, giving concrete examples of systemic causes of poverty (e.g., religious or gender discrimination, inadequate educational opportunities, political conflict and unrest).*

- Would your answer to this question be different for the materially poor in your own community versus a community abroad? Why or why not?

  —*Some participants may instinctually see individual choices as the root of poverty in your own community, but see structural circumstances as the source of poverty abroad. Move past these distinctions, focusing on both systems and choices in both contexts.*

  —*Help participants think about your own community in new ways: how educational systems are funded, how racial redlining has shaped neighborhoods and communities, etc.*

2. Look back at how you described the purpose of your trip in the preliminary questions. Did part of your stated purpose involve poverty alleviation?

- If so, given the ideas on poverty and poverty alleviation in this unit, how might you need to adjust your expectations?

3. Given the complexity of poverty and poverty alleviation, how can you specifically commit to make this trip one part of a long-term process of learning and engagement in God's work, rather than a one-

time spiritual or emotional experience? Take a moment to discuss what these commitments and goals might look like for your group.

—*Let participants know that they will continue to unpack these issues throughout the next months. They cannot fully answer these questions at this particular moment, but they will reference these initial reflections when creating post-field commitments.*

—*Thus, press participants to think of specific ideas, while also acknowledging that their answers will continue to evolve.*

—*Use this question to reinforce the idea that the "trip" is not the main thing— participants are entering a long-term process and journey.*

TAKEAWAYS

- Keep your eyes open for the ways poverty is influenced by broken relationships with God, self, others, and the rest of creation.

- Remember that poverty alleviation is not just a matter of providing people with material things. It is a process of reconciling the four foundational relationships. You are not participating in a short-term trip in order to directly alleviate poverty.

- View your trip as one piece of a long-term process of learning about, engaging with, and supporting God's work of missions and poverty alleviation.

CLOSE

Poverty is the result of broken relationships, and broken relationships can be restored by the work of Christ. He came to make all things new, breaking the hold of sin and death "far as the curse is found." He came to show us that we can have a relationship with our Father, that we have dignity as creatures made in God's image, that we are to love one another in nourishing community, and that we have the privilege of stewarding the rest of creation. The fall has marred what God intended for us at creation, but the work of Christ offers hope that what is broken, both inside of us and around us, will be repaired.

But that process doesn't happen in the space of a few days or weeks. If we are spending hundreds or thousands of dollars on a trip, we need a different set of goals, namely entering into a long-term, intentional process of learning about and engaging with what God is doing in our own country and around the globe—and supporting the people who *can* alleviate poverty in their own communities. It doesn't seem as tidy as digging wells, repairing houses, or running sports camps, but as we will see in the next few units, it can foster deeper change in both the receiving community and our own lives.

PRAY

"Every human being, regardless of income level, is made in the image of God, meaning that we are wired for relationship: with God, with ourselves, with others, and with the rest of creation. When we experience these four relationships in the way that God designed them, we experience humanness the way that He intended. This is the 'good life' that we are all seeking. Unfortunately, the fall has broken these four relationships for all people. For some, this brokenness manifests itself in material poverty."

Spend time this week praying that God would open your eyes to the complexity of poverty—and the magnitude of His reconciling power as He is making all things new. Pray that He would prepare your heart to see and support the work of your brothers and sisters who are already serving as ambassadors of reconciliation in their communities. And pray for humility as you consider what engaging with that work around the world and in your own community would look like.

NOTES

WHO ARE THE **POOR?**

Discuss this question before beginning this week's unit.

- Take a moment to reflect on a time when you helped a materially poor person. What was going through your mind during and after you helped this person? What do you imagine was going through their mind?

WHAT'S THE GOAL?

"We've been sent to the least of these." "Taking back Africa for Jesus." "Hope for New Orleans." The taglines appear on brochures, T-shirts, and fundraising letters. Images of malnourished children or homeless people sleeping under overpasses star in short-term trip promotional videos. The appeals are emotionally compelling, and appear to be built around the biblical mandate to care for the materially poor. But on a deeper level, they say an enormous amount about how we view ourselves and how we view low-income people. As we saw in unit 1, poverty is rooted in the complexity of broken relationships. Then who are the poor? And what does poverty alleviation look like?

WATCH

Close your books and watch this week's video via the QR code or link below.

 www.helpingwithouthurting.org/stm-videos

Follow the prompts to set up an account or sign back in, utilizing the access code below to view the videos:

Code: COL120

DISCUSS

Initial Reflections

1. What are two or three ideas that struck you in the video? What questions do you have after seeing the video?

OUR POVERTY

As discussed in the video, brokenness in the four relationships shapes all of us, not just the materially poor.

1. You may not be materially poor, but what evidence do you see in your life of brokenness in the four foundational relationships?

   • Relationship with God:

   • Relationship with Self:

   • Relationship with Others:

   • Relationship with the Rest of Creation:

Being aware of the way our own foundational relationships are marred by sin is crucial in fostering an attitude of humility. We are all dependent on the work of Christ in our lives, and we all share equal worth and value as His image-bearers. But as discussed in the video, the ways we experience poverty are fundamentally different. There is something uniquely devastating and painful about material poverty. The ways the materially rich experience poverty don't typically involve hunger pangs, watching family members die of malnutrition, or living in fear of violence outside our front doors. As we enter low-income communities, we must be very aware not to cheapen or delegitimize the pain that the materially poor endure by claiming to understand it, or that our experiences of brokenness are fully the same.

HELPING OR HURTING?

One of the biggest problems with short-term trips focused on poverty alleviation is that they can exacerbate the poverty of being of the economically rich—their god-complexes—and the poverty of being of the economically poor—their feelings of inferiority and shame.

Yes, we may help temporarily improve people's physical conditions. They may have clean water, repaired houses, or new classrooms. But other, powerful aspects of their poverty can be deepened. The equation below summarizes this dynamic:

Material Definition of Poverty	+	God-complexes of Materially Non-Poor	+	Feelings of Inferiority of Materially Poor	=	Harm to Both Materially Poor and Non-Poor

David Livermore, who has spent years studying cross-cultural engagement and short-term missions, shares a story that illustrates this dynamic. He and his wife, Linda, and their daughters were visiting Malaysia. After seeing a materially poor Malay father and daughter on the street, Livermore encouraged his own daughter to give the little girl a frog stuffed animal.

> As we started to leave, the Malay father ordered his daughter to return the frog. We motioned that we didn't want it back, but he insisted. He began to raise his voice and grabbed the frog and handed it to me. As I began to talk with Linda about it, we thought back to our home in the Chicago area. Though a beautiful house, our home was one of the more modest homes in our town. Linda asked, "So how would you feel if one of the parents in the million-dollar homes near us suddenly walked up to our girls and started handing them gifts?" All of a sudden I began to see this in a new light. I thought about how I would feel if some rich person started giving my girls unsolicited gifts in my presence. I'm quite capable of caring for them, thank you![1]

Livermore didn't anticipate that giving a simple stuffed animal—something he intended as an act of generosity—would provoke a negative response. Livermore's intentions were good, but he inadvertently angered and shamed the Malay father by implying that he could not adequately provide for his own child.

1. Have you ever seen this type of dynamic at work, whether in your own community or during a short-term trip? If so, how?

   —*If participants cannot think of an example specifically involving poverty alleviation, have them think of situations in other contexts—their families, schools, or workplaces—when they felt insulted by someone's attempts to help them.*

2. Look back at your answer to the preliminary question. In the situation you described, do you have any evidence to support what you think was going through the materially poor person's mind? How else might the materially poor recipient have perceived your help?

   Questions 3 and 4 should link back to participants' reflections on their own areas of brokenness in the previous section.

   —*Consider compiling individuals' answers to these questions and creating a composite list grouped thematically. Doing so will help you recognize any patterns in terms of what the group:*

   A) *Should be hopeful about—what are some opportunities for healing and growth?*

   B) *Should be careful of—what are areas of brokenness that the group needs to be collectively aware of, helping and supporting each other while they are on the field?*

   — *Additionally, let team members know that they will come back to these questions while they are on the field and in post-field reflection. Emphasize that healing—not despair or wallowing—is the goal.*

3. How might going on this trip help challenge you and heal you in areas of your brokenness?

4. How might going on this trip tempt you to further entrench areas of your brokenness?

TAKEAWAYS

- Remember that both the materially poor and materially rich experience brokenness in their four foundational relationships. You need Christ's reconciling work in your life, just as the materially poor do.

- Thus, remember that you are not going to "save" people who are poor. In fact, acting from a god-complex or arrogance-tainted heart is one of the fastest ways to harm the materially poor in our attempts to help them.

- Use Psalm 139:23–24 as an outline and central theme in prayer for this trip and learning process.

CLOSE

When we recognize that poverty is relational, *and that we are all poor,* we can enter a community with humility. We can guard against harming the materially poor with our god-complexes and arrogance, instead focusing our thoughts, actions, words, and attitudes on affirming the greatness of God, the dignity of the materially poor, and our mutual need for Christ. Rather than seeing ourselves as bringing hope to New Orleans or taking back Africa for Jesus, we can rejoice that Christ is already at work in these areas. Rather than seeing ourselves as saving "the least of these," we can celebrate together the ways the reconciling work of Christ is bringing healing to the poverty in *all of us*.

PRAY

"Who are the poor? We are the poor. When we truly believe this, when it shapes everything we say, think, and do, we can enter a materially poor community in humility. We can lay aside our drive to 'fix' the poor, we can put away our need to 'do' something, and instead we can open our hearts to learn from people who are poor, letting Christ restore both of us in our areas of brokenness."

Spend time praying together, reflecting on Psalm 139:23–24. Ask God to reveal the depths of your own sin and brokenness as you prepare for your trip. Pray that He would guard you against arrogance, using this process of learning and engagement to restore you to more of what He intended you to be.

NOTES

UNIT 3

THEY ARE NOT
HELPLESS

Discuss these questions before beginning this week's unit.

- In what contexts might you be willing to give low-income people things or money?

- In what contexts might you be uncomfortable giving low-income people things or money?

NOT ALL POVERTY IS CREATED EQUAL

After Hurricane Katrina wreaked havoc along parts of the Gulf Coast, tens of thousands of Christians rushed to assist, testifying to the beauty of the body of Christ. One particular youth short-term team arrived a few weeks after Katrina hit and cleared roads and homes of debris. The same group returned about a year later to help rehabilitate some of the damaged homes. The team spent days restoring a house owned by a family that included several young adult males. While the team worked hard every day tearing out Sheetrock, carpeting, and more, the young men living in the house sat back and watched the STM team. After the second trip, a few of the team members left unsettled—something didn't feel right. But why? Isn't all poverty created equal? After all, both trips were focused on serving the materially poor whom Hurricane Katrina had affected, and tasks and projects were successfully completed on both.

WATCH

Close your books and watch this week's video via the QR code or link below.

   www.helpingwithouthurting.org/stm-videos

Follow the prompts to set up an account or sign back in, utilizing the access code below to view the videos:

Code: COL120

DISCUSS

Initial Reflections

1. What are two or three ideas that struck you in the video? What questions do you have after seeing the video?

ONE OF THESE IS NOT LIKE THE OTHER

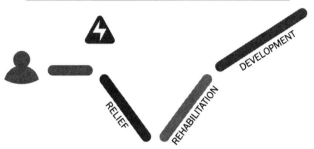

RELIEF, REHABILITATION, AND DEVELOPMENT

- **Relief**: An effort to "stop the bleeding." It is the urgent and temporary provision of emergency aid to reduce immediate suffering from a natural or man-made crisis, and it primarily utilizes a provider-receiver dynamic.

- **Rehabilitation**: An effort to restore people back to their pre-crisis state after the initial bleeding has stopped, while also laying the basis for future development. In rehabilitation, people begin to contribute to improving their situation.

- **Development**: Walking with people across time in ways that move all the people involved—both the "helpers" and the "helped"—closer to being in right relationship with God, self, others, and the rest of creation than they were before. This involves people identifying their problems, creating solutions, and implementing those solutions. Development is often referred to as "empowerment." It avoids "doing for" and focuses on "doing with."

Remember: The vast majority of materially poor communities and individuals require development, not relief or rehabilitation; they are not coming out of a crisis and they are not helpless. Rather, they are in a chronic state of poverty and have some ability to participate in their own progress.

Thus, a visual for development, which is the majority of poverty alleviation, is:

1. Look back at the preliminary questions to this unit. Would you retool your answers in light of the information about relief, rehabilitation, and development above? Why or why not?

> —*Explore whether participants see the appropriateness of handouts differently in their own community versus in a Majority World country.*

> —*Participants may view poverty abroad as so desperate that handouts are acceptable, while considering handouts of things or money harmful in their own communities.*

> —*If this is their perception, dig deeper into the basic assumptions about poverty and people who are poor in each context. Emphasize that even the vast majority of extremely poor communities need development.*

IS THE GLASS HALF EMPTY OR HALF FULL?

1. Read the following verses. How might these verses inform the way we interact with the materially poor?

- 1 Thessalonians 5:10–11:

• Philippians 4:8:

• 1 Corinthians 12:12–26:

No division, one body, members one to another, orient yourself to your position, function as you want to be willing to accept + engage them.

• James 2:1–5:

Review the definitions of asset-based and needs-based development below.

NEEDS-BASED DEVELOPMENT

A development approach that focuses on the deficits and shortcomings in the life of a person or community; solutions to individual or community problems come from the outside

ASSET-BASED DEVELOPMENT

A development approach that focuses on identifying, mobilizing, and connecting the God-given capabilities, skills, and resources of a person or community to solve individual or community problems

Healthy, effective poverty alleviation approaches start by recognizing and celebrating the gifts and resources God has already placed in a community, whether natural resources, people, families, neighborhood associations, schools, businesses, governments, or individual skills. This isn't ignoring the problems that exist, but rather it is recognizing that there are assets available within a community and its people to attack the problems and create new opportunities. The exciting process of asset-based development is focused on identifying, mobilizing, and connecting these assets.

THE POISON OF PATERNALISM

Paternalism is habitually doing things for people that they can do for themselves.[1] Paternalism is slippery, though. It isn't just a matter of inappropriate handouts—it takes a number of subtle forms. Note the following variations of paternalism:

What ever do I have Most?

- **Resource Paternalism**: giving people resources they do not truly need and/or could acquire on their own

- **Spiritual Paternalism**: taking spiritual leadership away from the materially poor, assuming we have more to offer than they do

- **Knowledge Paternalism**: assuming we have all the best ideas about how to do things

- **Labor Paternalism**: doing work for the materially poor that they could do for themselves

- **Managerial Paternalism**: taking ownership of change away from the poor, insisting that they follow our "better, "more efficient" way of doing things

1. While you may have never experienced material poverty, consider experiences in your job, school, home, or church. Have you ever been on the receiving end of spiritual, managerial, or knowledge paternalism? How did those experiences make you feel?

2. Why do you think people are so quick to engage in paternalism, despite its negative effects?

  —*Discuss the emotional draw of "doing" something and the nature of our own brokenness (e.g., god-complexes, arrogance.)*

3. Given the context of poverty that you will be experiencing on this visit, what type of asset-based interventions is the host ministry doing?

  —*By this time, you should have specific information about existing assets in the community and your field host's work. Review these ministries and assets with the participants, broadly discussing what makes this work asset-based rather than needs-based.*

4. What actions by your group could support their success?

  —*Listen to people, whether the host or community members, describe the kinds of resources and assets they have in their community.*

  —*Encourage local people and workers, and celebrate stories of how their assets have been used in the past and will be used in the future.*

5. What actions by your group could hinder their success?

—*Begin this discussion by recognizing the causes of poverty in the community and whether the context requires relief, rehabilitation, or development.*

—*Remind participants that unless a person or community is coming out of an immediate crisis, relief-style handouts and paternalism hinder effective poverty alleviation and harm the local economy. Discuss what avoiding the different forms of paternalism might look like in your particular context.*

—*Utilize specific, applied scenarios like those in chapter 8, page 116, of the Leader's Guide, unpacking how to appropriately handle potentially difficult situations.*

—*Note: If you will be contributing your labor alongside community members on a locally led project, utilize pages 81–82 of the* Leader's Guide *to introduce participants to the circumstances in which contributing to a task can be healthy.*

6. How might you specifically hold each other accountable to support, rather than hinder, successful ministry on this visit?

CLOSE

Not all poverty is created equal. Clearing debris after a hurricane and renovating houses for people a year later may seem like similarly valid responses to poverty. But context is everything. We have a responsibility to not harm a community when we enter it, and to not undermine the long-term poverty alleviation work already being done. We love *doing* things, and we forget that the materially poor are not helpless. There are times when more or less assistance is needed. But they are ultimately created in the image of God with unique gifts and capacities. We dare not rob them of that dignity through our efforts to do and accomplish particular tasks. Instead, as we will explore in the following units, we have an opportunity to learn from them and affirm their dignity through short-term trips.

TAKEAWAYS

- Do not give money or material things to the people you encounter. If you desire to help, then approach the host organization and allow them to determine how the resources can be best used.

- Avoid paternalism; do not do things for the materially poor that they are capable of doing for themselves. You may have opportunities to work *alongside* community members on a task that they have initiated and are executing, blessing them with your company and additional labor. But involvement should always be under their leadership and participation.

- Rather than fixating on the material needs you see, look for the gifts God has already placed in the community and in individuals.

PRAY

"If you go back to the definition of poverty, poverty alleviation isn't just about fixing the materially poor's circumstances. It is about helping them discover that they are an image-bearer and that they have tremendous value as a human being, that they are called to be a steward of their resources and opportunities. When we visit a community, we have to be incredibly careful that we respect that process, not undermine it."

Pray for the work that God is already doing in the community you will be visiting. Pray that God would give you open eyes and hearts to recognize that work and to see the gifts He has given the materially poor. Ask for wisdom as you enter the community, coming alongside your brothers and sisters as they engage in the long-term process of poverty alleviation.

NOTES

UNIT 4

THE KINGDOM IS
UPSIDE **DOWN**

Discuss these questions before beginning this week's unit.

- Has there ever been a time when someone sought out your wisdom or opinion, wanting to learn from your experiences? How did this make you feel? Yes - valued and respected.

- Has there ever been a time when someone was willing to enter into your life, listening to you share aspects of your heart and reality? How did this make you feel? Yes - Old John. It makes me feel cared for and valued.

WHAT NOW?

If poverty alleviation is a long-term process and can't be achieved by simply providing material things to people who are poor, then what is the purpose of a short-term trip? If trips focused on "doing" or "fixing" things often cause harm, then on what are we called to focus? Consider the following story from David Livermore:

> A group from my church just returned from a couple weeks in Rwanda. Within their first hour in Rwanda, the local team said, "Ninety percent of your job is done. You're here, your presence speaks volumes." One of the team members told me she thought, "Well, I don't think so. That's gracious of you, but we're here to work hard." The longer she was there, however, the more she began to see that the tasks they came to do were not what was needed most. The presence and chance for relationship together seemed to be the most pressing need for the Rwandan church beyond any menial tasks that were planned.[1]

When done well, a short-term trip is just one step in the long-term process of Jesus Christ remaking both the materially poor and those of us who want to help. Within that framework, our presence can be a powerful blessing, and what we learn during our time can create opportunities for transformation down the road.

WATCH

Close your books and watch this week's video via the QR code or link below.

 www.helpingwithouthurting.org/stm-videos

Follow the prompts to set up an account or sign back in, utilizing the access code below to view the videos:

Code: COL120

DISCUSS

Initial Reflections

1. What are two or three ideas that struck you in the video? What questions do you have after seeing the video?

   The Emphesis on learning struk out to me most of all.

WHAT LEARNING, FELLOWSHIP, AND ENCOURAGEMENT CAN LOOK LIKE

1. Read 1 Corinthians 1:26–31 and Colossians 4:7–16. How might these passages provide a foundation for engaging in learning, fellowship, and encouragement as we enter a low-income community?

   Not many of us are wise. But God uses the foolish to engage this culture.

   • Now think back to the ways the materially poor and non-poor are broken. How could entering a community with a 1 Corinthians 1 attitude begin to address the brokenness in both of our hearts?

   —*Emphasize that this attitude affirms the dignity of the materially poor (combating any sense of shame or inferiority on their part) and challenges our arrogance (our god-complexes and sense of superiority.)*

The idea that learning, fellowship, and encouragement are legitimate purposes for a short-term trip within the context of long-term engagement can seem strange at first. Take a moment to read the accounts below:

Our groups would sit on an open-air porch around a single table for dinner, and various members of the community would join us four or five times throughout the week. The guests were very different—farmers, pastors, students, or housewives. One at a time, they would eat with us and we would all swap stories and small talk. After supper, they would share about their worlds. The teacher would talk about the educational challenges in the community. The pastor would talk about spiritual warfare. The student would explain his or her typical day, how he or she would walk three to four miles to school or do homework by candlelight. . . . Other times, we would arrange for team members to attend church services that just met in community members' front yards. We wanted participants to see and understand how the local church was already proclaiming God's excellencies and ministering to one another.

—Michael and Shelley, former full-time missionaries[2]

I was leading a team of youth on a short-term trip to a very secular part of Europe. We had anticipated the primary focus being projects on the church building, or outreach to the low-income community around the church. Instead, when we got there, the pastor greeted the team and said, "All I care about is that you have breakfast, lunch, and dinner with members of our church every day. This isn't the easiest place to be a Christian—there aren't tons of passionate believers around us. I want your presence and passion to be refreshing to our church." At first, I found the notion strange. Eating meals with church members? But then I realized, "What a beautiful example of what a short-term trip can be."

—Marco Perez, former team leader and team host[3]

The following story is from Jason, who has led trips as part of long-term engagement with orphans, many of whom are now young adults:

I never understood the place of lament in our faith [before]. One night during a praise service, several of the youth just broke down crying, and then doubled over screaming. They began sobbing, "Why, why, why," and "It hurts, it hurts, it hurts," and "Why did they leave me?" It was gut-wrenching. We didn't know how to process that. It sent us, as a team and congregation, on years of exploring what worship looks like out of a context of pain and distress. None of that was in the gospel that we consciously brought with us to that community. But it is a part of the gospel that the Spirit led us to through our relationships with them. We read our Bibles, especially the Psalms, in new ways. . . . Because of these types of encounters, some participants have even pursued formal training in trauma therapy and counseling. They are now using that training in our own community and as we continue to walk alongside our brothers and sisters overseas.[4]

1. What strikes you about the underlying values and attitudes expressed in these stories and quotes?

   —*Link this discussion back to the attitude displayed in 1 Corinthians 1: we are all dependent on God's work, the "weak" of the world have much to teach us, etc.*

2. How do you feel now about having learning, fellowship, and encouragement as the core purposes of this visit?

   —*Spend significant time on this question. The goal is to see team members embrace the value of learning, fellowship, and encouragement as legitimate purposes for the trip.*

   —*If they do not embrace these goals, ask, "Why not?"*

   —*If you breeze through this question, thinking that participants accept these purposes when they do not, it could cause difficult, damaging situations during the trip; participants will naturally revert to "doing."*

TAKEAWAYS

• You must be committed to learning about the historical, social, political, and spiritual context of the community you will be visiting, and seek to better understand the complex causes and manifestations of poverty in the area.

• During this visit, be ready to look for specific ways that you can learn from the materially poor's experiences and wisdom. Be open to ways God may use them to confront or address areas of sin and brokenness in your own heart.

• Remember: as you learn from and fellowship with your brothers and sisters, constantly consider what your long-term role is in engaging with and supporting effective poverty alleviation and missions—both around the world and in your own community.

CLOSE

God does not call His children because they are exceptional. He does not choose the perfect, the wealthy, or the influential. No one has grounds to boast, and none of us are at the "top" in His kingdom. When we enter a low-income community and prioritize learning, fellowship, and encouragement, we are recognizing that God chooses the "foolish things of the world to shame the wise" and "the weak things of the world to shame the strong" (1 Corinthians 1:27). Instead of focusing on accomplishing projects and tasks, we enter into a refrain of humble praise: "Let us boast in the Lord together! Let us celebrate the things He has done in our lives through Christ!" In the process, we leave our hearts open to Christ as He remakes us, leading us toward long-term, deeply transformative ways of joining in His work.

PRAY

"When we pause, setting the shovels down and putting the puppets away, we realize that the materially poor have an incredible amount to teach us about God, the kingdom, and ourselves. In return, we have the privilege of humbly coming alongside the work God is doing through them, supporting them and engaging with them in work that we could never do as outsiders. And that's a beautiful thing."

Spend time in prayer, asking God to give you a heart of profound humility and openness to what He has for you to learn. And pray that He would give you sensitivity to how you can best bless and encourage His people working in the community, loving your brothers and sisters well.

NOTES

UNIT 5

BEING A **BLESSING**

Discuss these questions before beginning this week's unit.

• Describe a time when someone misunderstood your words or actions. What was at the root of the misunderstanding?

• Describe a time when you felt disrespected by someone. Why did you feel this way?

DANCING CAREFULLY

As we build trips around learning, fellowship, and encouragement, we still have to be very conscientious when interacting with our hosts. Missions expert Miriam Adeney relates a story told to her by an African Christian friend:

> Elephant and Mouse were best friends. One day Elephant said, "Mouse, let's have a party!" Animals gathered from far and near. They ate, and drank, and sang, and danced. And nobody celebrated more exuberantly than the Elephant. After it was over, Elephant exclaimed, "Mouse, did you ever go to a better party? What a celebration!" But Mouse did not answer. "Where are you?" Elephant called. Then he shrank back in horror. There at his feet lay the Mouse, his body ground into the dirt—smashed by the exuberance of his friend, the Elephant. "Sometimes that is what it is like to do mission with you Westerners," the African storyteller commented. "It is like dancing with an Elephant."[1]

Thankfully, there are ways we can prepare to dance well during our visits, seeking to support and bless our hosts more effectively.

WATCH

Close your books and watch this week's video via the QR code or link below.

 www.helpingwithouthurting.org/stm-videos

Follow the prompts to set up an account or sign back in, utilizing the access code below to view the videos:

Code: COL120

DISCUSS

Initial Reflections

1. What are two or three ideas that struck you in the video? What questions do you have after seeing the video?

NO SUCH THING AS "NORMAL"

1. Review the definition of "cultural norms" below.

> ## CULTURAL NORMS
>
> Subconscious assumptions, behaviors, and protocols that people naturally follow without even thinking about them

2. Have you ever personally encountered a different set of cultural norms, whether in another country, another church, or even another family setting? If so, how did you respond?

3. Referencing resource module B, your leader will now talk you through some of the basic differences in the cultural norms below. What three norms appear to pose the biggest difference between your culture and the receiving culture?

- Concept of Time:

- Concept of Self:

- Role of Face/Degree of Directness:

- Locus of Control:

- Power Distance:

  —*Utilize material from chapter 4 of the Leader's Guide, and have partici-pants reference resource module B.*

  —*After completing this unit and before entering the field, you will need to pro-vide the team with cultural training specific to the receiving community. If you are going through an intermediary organization, it should provide some basic materials.*

4. Take a moment to imagine a situation in which a differing norm could cause problems or present challenges on your trip. How might you handle this situation wisely, respecting your hosts?

5. What might be the implications of the following passages on respecting our brothers and sisters and respecting cultural differences?

• Philippians 2:1–11:

• Ephesians 4:1–6:

—*Strike a balance between:*

A) *Participants thinking that "different" can never be "wrong," denying that biblical standards of behavior or truth bridge cultures.*

B) *Participants assuming that everything about their culture flows from biblical directives, mistaking elements of culture for prescriptive biblical standards.*

—*Communicate that "different" is not automatically wrong or right. Sometimes people from different cultures can be obeying the same biblical principle, but the way they act it out looks very different.*

—*Thus, encourage participants to avoid immediately judging negatively what they do not understand.*

LEAVING DONALD AT HOME

When we, as middle-to-upper-class people, walk into a low-income community—particularly in the Majority World—everything we say carries more weight than we intend. As a result, we can undermine local participation and initiative in development and ministry work. It also means that our displeasure or frustrations can be magnified, causing extra insult and damage.

1. Have you ever been on the receiving end of the Donald Trump Effect, whether in your church, office, or family?

2. Have you ever been pushed toward a particular action because of someone's resources, influence, or status? If so, how did it make you feel?

   —*Lead people to share some of these negative experiences, and help them see how receiving communities/organizations might feel the same way if teams are not mindful visitors.*

3. Are you mentally, emotionally, and spiritually prepared to take a backseat to local workers and believers, supporting their work at the expense of a feeling of contributing to helping people who are poor?

PICTURING DIGNITY

We live in a culture where every latte, sunset, or family gathering is fair game for a picture or social media post. For many of us, it is a way of sharing and documenting our day-to-day lives. But we need to be aware of how our love for photography and social media may play out on a short-term trip. Take a moment to discuss the following questions:

   —*See chapters 7 and 9, pages 104 and 124 of the Leader's Guide for your own review on appropriate use of images and social media.*

   —*In this section, explain what your policies for social media use will be (particularly if you are prohibiting it entirely)*

1. How would you feel if you were walking in your neighborhood and someone drove by taking pictures of you?

2. What if a stranger walked into your church and started taking pictures of your children, nieces or nephews, or younger siblings, posting these pictures on the Internet for the world to see? How would you feel?

When we enter a low-income community, we have to adjust our habits and ask ourselves whether we are "doing unto others" well. The stories we are hearing and the scenes we are seeing aren't ours to share with the rest of the world automatically. We have to respect the dignity and privacy of the people we encounter, including through our photography. A picture of a hurting, vacant-eyed mother may be emotionally compelling, but it doesn't prioritize her dignity. A picture of you with malnourished, needy-looking children may make for a great profile pic, but it can treat those children and families as a spectacle. Before you snap a picture, ask yourself the following questions:

• Does this picture communicate and emphasize the God-given gifts and dignity of the materially poor, or does it flatten them into a one-dimensional caricature of pain and desperation?

• Does this picture paint me as saving, rescuing, or fixing the materially poor or their community in any way?

• How would I feel if outsiders depicted me or my community in this way? Am I "doing unto others" well?

Further, your trip leader may prohibit social media use while you are on the field. Be fully present, setting aside the desire to document a moment in favor of creating a safe space for personal interaction. Live in the rhythm of the community, removing the mental and emotional distraction of keeping up with home. Your trip leader can and will keep your families updated. So unplug. You will learn more if you do.

Here are a few general guidelines to follow while you are on the field:

• Do not take pictures during conversations, worship gatherings, or visiting someone's home.

• Ask permission before taking pictures of or with people, and be extremely cautious of taking pictures of or with children.

• If you do use social media during the trip, limit it to evenings and run a draft post by a team member, discussing whether it is dignity-affirming or not.

TAKEAWAYS

• Assume things are more complex than meets the eye. Be very slow to make assumptions about people, situations, attitudes, or problems.

• Carefully listen to and obey instructions from your local hosts, respecting their procedures, behavioral guidelines, and cultural advice.

• Be flexible. Recognize that plans and logistics during your trip will most likely change or be upended at a moment's notice. Be prepared to go with the flow, rather than expecting things to go a certain way.

• Be extremely hesitant to make "suggestions" or share your opinions. Remember: your hosts know more about living in their communities than you ever could. You are not the experts.

- Be very cautious about photography and social media usage. "Do unto others" well.

CLOSE

Visiting a new context and culture can be disorienting and overwhelming, particularly if we feel the pressure to accomplish something or have a particular experience. As we have discussed, moving away from an emphasis on "doing" allows us to dance well on short-term trips, reframing the visit as an opportunity to learn from, fellowship with, and encourage our hosts. But more than anything, remember that your trip is one piece in a long-term process of learning and engagement. Don't feel pressure to have a profound experience each day. Don't force an incident or story to have immediate meaning. Yes, be thoughtful and observant. But remember: snap judgments and assumptions typically lead us to faulty conclusions.

You will record your experiences throughout your trip in unit 6. You will then reflect on and analyze those experiences when you return home, setting concrete goals about how you will steward your trip and engage as you move forward. So take the long view, and don't expect the trip itself to be a revolutionary experience. In fact, by itself, the trip probably will not create concrete, lasting change in your life. It's what you do when you return, and the ongoing work of the Holy Spirit, that fosters long-term growth and transformation.

PRAY

"Ultimately, we have a responsibility to 'do unto others' well. Yes, these kinds of contextual and cultural differences can complicate that process. But that's why we start with listening. We start with learning. We start with just being with our brothers and sisters. And we trust that God will work in and through that process, opening new, mutually edifying ways for us to serve and to support one another."

Pray that God would grant you and your team wisdom as you enter an unfamiliar community. Pray that He would give you sensitivity to opportunities to effectively bless the people you meet, and that He would prompt your heart at any moments where your own god-complexes might be tainting those interactions.

NOTES

UNIT 6

ON THE **GROUND**[1]

Most of the questions in unit 6 are meant for reflection, so responses will be personal; you will not be leading participants to set conclusions. However, there will be some scripting for the Final Evening Reflection Questions.

OBSERVATION CATEGORIES

Skim over the topics below each evening, jotting down any stories or observations that relate to these ideas. You will return to these observations after your trip to think about and discuss them further. Don't feel like you need to write an essay each night. Use brief bullet points or keywords. Think of the below categories as buckets to help gather and sort your experiences, ensuring that you don't forget the things you observed.

• Different aspects of broken relationships and material poverty

- Examples of effective and ineffective poverty alleviation (healthy development work vs. inappropriate relief efforts, the materially poor participating in their own improvement vs. the temptations and dangers of paternalism, etc.)

- Seeing the materially poor through the lens of their God-given gifts and assets, not their needs or deficits

- The beauty of learning from, fellowshiping with, and encouraging our brothers and sisters, even those the world would call "weak"

• Respecting the culture and leaders of the receiving community

• Learning about and recognizing the systemic causes of poverty, such as economic, social, or political factors, in a particular area.

TRACKING QUESTIONS

Each evening, take a moment to look at the questions below. Using bullet points, jot down answers under the questions. Expand on your thoughts and stories as much as you would like, but don't feel pressure to write long paragraphs. You will return to these observations later.

Date:

1. Briefly recap your day. How did you spend your time, and with whom did you interact?

2. What was the highlight of your day—what was the most exciting, interesting, or energizing moment?

3. What was the hardest part of your day—what was the most saddening, confusing, or frustrating moment?

4. Did today's experiences leave you with any: A) Questions or areas you would like to understand more deeply? or B) Ideas about how you can engage with and support poverty alleviation as you return home?

Date:

1. Briefly recap your day. How did you spend your time, and with whom did you interact?

2. What was the highlight of your day—what was the most exciting, interesting, or energizing moment?

3. What was the hardest part of your day—what was the most saddening, confusing, or frustrating moment?

4. Did today's experiences leave you with any: A) Questions or areas you would like to understand more deeply? or B) Ideas about how you can engage with and support poverty alleviation as you return home?

Date:

1. Briefly recap your day. How did you spend your time, and with whom did you interact?

2. What was the highlight of your day—what was the most exciting, interesting, or energizing moment?

3. What was the hardest part of your day—what was the most saddening, confusing, or frustrating moment?

4. Did today's experiences leave you with any: A) Questions or areas you would like to understand more deeply? or B) Ideas about how you can engage with and support poverty alleviation as you return home?

Date:

1. Briefly recap your day. How did you spend your time, and with whom did you interact?

2. What was the highlight of your day—what was the most exciting, interesting, or energizing moment?

3. What was the hardest part of your day—what was the most saddening, confusing, or frustrating moment?

4. Did today's experiences leave you with any: A) Questions or areas you would like to understand more deeply? or B) Ideas about how you can engage with and support poverty alleviation as you return home?

Date:

1. Briefly recap your day. How did you spend your time, and with whom did you interact?

2. What was the highlight of your day—what was the most exciting, interesting, or energizing moment?

3. What was the hardest part of your day—what was the most saddening, confusing, or frustrating moment?

4. Did today's experiences leave you with any: A) Questions or areas you would like to understand more deeply? or B) Ideas about how you can engage with and support poverty alleviation as you return home?

Date:

1. Briefly recap your day. How did you spend your time, and with whom did you interact?

2. What was the highlight of your day—what was the most exciting, interesting, or energizing moment?

3. What was the hardest part of your day—what was the most saddening, confusing, or frustrating moment?

4. Did today's experiences leave you with any: A) Questions or areas you would like to understand more deeply? or B) Ideas about how you can engage with and support poverty alleviation as you return home?

Date:

1. Briefly recap your day. How did you spend your time, and with whom did you interact?

2. What was the highlight of your day—what was the most exciting, interesting, or energizing moment?

3. What was the hardest part of your day—what was the most saddening, confusing, or frustrating moment?

4. Did today's experiences leave you with any: A) Questions or areas you would like to understand more deeply? or B) Ideas about how you can engage with and support poverty alleviation as you return home?

FINAL EVENING REFLECTIONS[2]

During your final group meeting on the field, spend time discussing the below questions.

1. Jot down what you would consider the top two highlights of this trip. What made these highlights?

2. Reflect on what the most difficult part of this trip was for you. Why do you think it was so hard?

3. What are some ways you can continue the process of learning and engagement when you return home, supporting the work you visited and effective poverty alleviation in your own community? Jot down some initial goals for how you will steward this experience, making it one piece of a long-term process. You will revisit these goals when you return home, but for now, share the first few things that come to mind.

   —*Point people back to their answers in the final question of unit 1.*

   —*Be sure that you leave adequate time for this question. Again, how people set goals and move forward makes all the difference in translating a visit into lasting impact.*

4. When people ask you about your trip when you return home, what will you tell them? Take several minutes to write a couple of sentences describing the purpose of the trip, what you learned, and how you will now be exploring what deeper engagement in effective poverty alleviation might look like.

> —*Encourage participants to focus on ideas that people back home might not typically hear from returning team members.*

> —*Help them move away from common and generic statements like, "They were wonderful people and they were so happy," or "I left totally changed."*

> —*Help them emphasize ongoing engagement with the work they visited, communicating that their work is not finished because the trip is over. Suggest statements like: "It's not done. In some ways it's just beginning."*

5. What are specific ways your team can pray for you as you return home? Take time to pray for each other, the community you have visited, the brothers and sisters you have met, and the work that God is doing.

6. Look over unit 7, and begin thinking about how you would respond to those questions. Before your first post-trip meeting, jot down your thoughts in unit 7, preparing to share your ideas with your team.

NOTES

UNIT 7

UNPACKING

As with unit 6, many of the answers to the questions in unit 7 are personal. There-fore, there is little scripting below.

OPEN

• Take a moment and share what you have felt and experienced as you have returned home. Are there moments that you have found awk-ward or difficult? If so, how and why?

• Is there a particular moment or person on your trip that you have found yourself thinking of more than any other? If so, share it.

REFLECT

Jot down basic thoughts to the following questions before coming to your first post-trip meeting. At the meeting, share your ideas, referencing your on-field journaling to inform your discussion.

UNDERSTANDING POVERTY ALLEVIATION

1. What struck you or surprised you about what effective poverty alleviation looks like on a practical level? Were there elements of poverty alleviation that were more complex than you realized before your trip?

2. Reflect on the work of the organization or ministry that hosted your team. In what ways did you see the principles of asset-based, participatory development at work?

3. Did you see any paternalism evident in your own heart and actions? If so, how did you go about addressing it during the course of the trip?

• Did you see any paternalism at work in the broader community you visited? If so, what forms (labor, resource, knowledge, spiritual, and/or managerial) did you observe?

LEARNING FROM THE MATERIALLY POOR

1. What personal, spiritual, physical, and social assets or strengths did you see in the local community?

• In what ways did your presence support and celebrate the God-given gifts in the community?

2. How did you specifically and deliberately submit to the leadership of the local leaders?

• Were there any moments when you struggled to respect and follow the direction of your hosts? If so, when and why? How did you navigate those moments?

3. Reflect on your interactions with local people. What did you learn from their experiences and stories? What challenged you? What encouraged you?

4. Think back to your times of fellowship with local believers. Did spending time with your brothers and sisters impact the way you view your faith, the church, and/or the kingdom of God? If so, how?

UNDERSTANDING THEIR WORLD

1. What cultural differences did you encounter during your visit? Were there any tense moments because of cultural differences, particularly regarding the cultural norms you studied before your trip?

• If so, how did you navigate these moments?

• What strengths did you see in the receiving community's culture?

2. In what ways did you see individual choices contributing to poverty in the receiving community? In what ways did you see systemic factors—circumstances outside of the control of a materially poor person—contribute to poverty?

3. Reflect on poverty in your own community. Are there any ways in which your experience on your trip might inform the way you view the materially poor in your own context?

   —*Take time on this question. A trip can and should help people see ways that they need to be more engaged in their own community. Challenge participants to begin translating what they learned to their context.*

PROCESSING MUTUAL POVERTY

1. In what ways did the trip reveal areas of brokenness in your own four relationships?

2. What might it look like for you to more fully rely on Christ's reconciling work in your life in these areas?

CLOSE

The visit you just experienced was a gift. The world has shrunk remarkably in the space of a few decades, creating new opportunities to engage with the body of Christ and see the work God is doing through His people. The apostle Paul spent his life sailing around the Mediterranean world visiting churches, often arriving shipwrecked, waterlogged, or snakebitten. Early believers, or even the missionaries of 150 years ago, could never have dreamed of boarding an airplane or bus and traveling as freely and easily as you just did. *But more than a gift, this trip was an investment.* God has entrusted you with this opportunity. So embrace your responsibility to continue the process of learning and engagement. Move forward with a humble heart, seeking how and where God would have you apply this experience to your heart and in your own community.

PRAY

"Search me, God, and know my heart;
   test me and know my anxious thoughts.
See if there is any offensive way in me,
   and lead me in the way everlasting."

—Psalm 139:23-24

Spend time in prayer, asking God to continually reveal areas of your heart in need of His healing work. And pray for humility and perseverance, asking God to give you a teachable heart as you consider what applying and stewarding this experience looks like.

NOTES

UNIT 8

MAKING IT **COUNT**

Discuss the following questions before beginning this week's unit.

- Take a moment to reflect once more on all that your trip cost. What was the monetary cost? How much time did members of the receiving community dedicate to hosting you?

- Two years from now, how would you like to answer the following question: "How did your visit lead to positive change in materially poor communities?"

IT ISN'T OVER

You prepared for your trip well. You did your best to learn from, respect, and encourage your hosts. But a few simple facts remain: An international short-term trip costs an average of $1,370–$1,450 per person.[1] The range of *yearly* salary for a community-level relief and development worker in the Majority World is $3,000–6,000. That means the money spent on a team of fifteen people could support three to seven local staff members for a year. One missionary, when asked about the amount of time it takes to prepare, host, and recover from hosting a team, estimated that it took four weeks of work time.[2]

Your job isn't done yet. How will you steward and build upon the dollars, hours, and effort *invested in you*? How will you allow your experience to shape the way you engage with God's work in the world and with your materially poor brothers and sisters? While the Holy Spirit is the ultimate author of change in our hearts, we have a responsibility to be active participants in that process. So how will you make this experience count?

WATCH

Close your books and watch this week's video via the QR code or link below.

www.helpingwithouthurting.org/stm-videos

Follow the prompts to set up an account or sign back in, utilizing the access code below to view the videos:

Code: COL120

DISCUSS

Initial Reflections

1. What are two or three ideas that struck you in the video? What questions do you have after seeing the video?

MAKING A CHANGE

1. Take a moment to read Philippians 2:4–13. What might this passage say about how we should view obedience and the process of change in our lives?

In light of these truths, take a moment to review the list of possible avenues for long-term engagement below:

• **Pray** faithfully for the community and people you visited, for your own community, and for wisdom as you continue to learn about and engage in God's work in the world.

• **Advocate** for the specific ministry or organization you visited, telling others the story of what God is doing. As part of this process, stay connected with the region and community you visited via newsletters from the host organization and broader current events that impact the community.

• **Financially support** the specific ministry or organization you visited, enabling them to continue ministering in their own community.

- **Support effective ministry** in your own community through your prayers, finances, time, and encouragement.

- **Support the leadership** of your church as they develop healthy partnerships and engage in effective poverty alleviation both in your own community and around the world.

- **Be a loving voice** in your congregation for effective poverty alleviation approaches.

2. Can you think of any other things you would add to the list above? If so, what?

3. Look back at the initial goals you described on your last day on the field (end of unit 6.) In light of those goals, your answer to the second preliminary question, and the list above, discuss three ways you might more deeply engage with and support what God is doing.

4. One of the most important factors in implementing change is setting effective goals. A common acronym for goal-setting is SMART. This means goals should be Specific, Measurable, Area-specific, Realistic, and Time-bound. Building on your answers above, write out two SMART goals for further engagement. For each goal, commit to steps and time frames below.

   —*This particular exercise may be the single most important step so far in the learning and engagement process. Be sure you set aside plenty of time for it.*

—If you cannot complete this step in one meeting, you may have to extend it to another gathering.

• In the next two months, I will:

• In the next six months, I will:

• In the next year, I will:

5. You will be meeting monthly or bimonthly to check in with your group. But take a moment to discuss how you might specifically hold each other accountable to these goals between meetings.

   —Discuss practical ways of maintaining contact: text messages, creating an invite-only Facebook group as a space for people to share their thoughts and progress, selecting prayer partners, etc.

POTENTIAL HANG-UPS

Take a moment to review the list of obstacles short-term trip participants often face following their experience:

- Putting their experience on the shelf, leaving it to be a one-time emotional or spiritual high

- Becoming an STM consumer, taking repeated trips to enjoy the spiritual high without implementing change in their daily lives

- Becoming arrogant, thinking that they are superior to others because of what they have seen, learned, or experienced

1. Are there any other obstacles that you can imagine encountering? If so, what?

2. Of the obstacles above, which do you think will be particularly tempting or problematic for you?

- What steps could you take to guard yourself from experiencing this obstacle, and how can your team pray for you in that process?

REPORTING BACK

You have a responsibility to communicate to your prayer and financial supporters how you are stewarding their investment. Create a follow-up letter to send to these supporters that answers the following questions:

• What are the things you are learning as a result of this long-term process?

• What were some of the ways that you supported and encouraged your hosts while you were there?

• What was the highlight of the visit, and what was the most stretching part of the visit?

• What are the specific steps you are taking and seeking to take in order to convert this experience into lasting change in your life and ongoing engagement with God's work?

• What ways can your supporters continue to pray for you and the community you visited?

1. Discuss as a team the date by which you will send this letter to your supporters.

—*Emphasize that the tone of this letter should be very humble, giving supporters a glimpse of what God did/is doing through the visit and learning process. This is not an opportunity to judge or arrogantly state how others need to change.*

At your next team meeting, you will hold each other accountable for writing and sending this letter. Further, if you are presenting anything to your church about this journey, use the above questions as an outline for your presentation.

NEXT STEPS SUMMARY

Compile your reflections above into a concrete plan.

1. I am committing to stay engaged in the work I saw and what God is doing in my own community by:

2. The top obstacle I need to be aware of as I pursue these goals is:

3. I will send my follow-up letter to supporters by:

4. Our next check-in meeting as a team is on:

TAKEAWAYS

- Return to your "Next Steps Summary" on a weekly or biweekly basis, reminding yourself of the goals you created for ongoing engagement.

- Keep in touch with your team members, encouraging and holding each other accountable for stewarding your experiences and following through on your goals.

- Pray that God would grant you perseverance, focus, and diligence in the process of stewarding your trip, remembering that God is the one who is ultimately at work in your heart.

CLOSE

Over the past several months, you have learned about the principles of poverty alleviation, the beauty of culture, and what God is doing in another community. You have traveled to see that work, to meet with your brothers and sisters, and explore how you can best love and support them. And hopefully God has opened your eyes to your own need of Him, leaving you with an incredible longing for His reconciling power to heal the brokenness in and around you.

Foster that longing and join that work. Jesus Christ is indeed making all things new, and it is our great privilege to be part of that process. Remember that you aren't alone in longing for glimpses of Christ's ultimate restoration to invade the brokenness of this world, for the good news of the gospel to be proclaimed and demonstrated among people who are poor. The brothers and sisters you visited, and the very people sitting next to you, stand with you in that longing. And most importantly, that longing itself is the Spirit working in and through you.

Day by day and year by year, dig deeper in to the depth and breadth of God's work in the world. Build on what you have experienced, using it as a catalyst for your own transformation and the transformation of others. Steward the opportunity well, and rejoice that God is faithful to complete what He has begun.

PRAY

"What happens as you move forward is the single biggest factor in whether your trip was worth it. You just encountered both the pain of material poverty and hopefully the beauty of Christ's reconciling work in a new way. But you know that this excitement of the experience of the trip itself will be short-lived. Change happens when we prayerfully and purposefully convert your trip experience into a deep joy about the kingdom of God and the privilege it is to be a part of His work in the world."

Spend time in prayer for the community you visited and for the brothers and sisters you encountered. Pray that God would give you the endurance to pursue lasting engagement with His work, resting in the power of the Holy Spirit to bring forth fruit in your life.

CHECKING IN

Use these questions during your monthly or bimonthly accountability and encouragement meetings.

1. Have you had any new reflections, insights, or questions about your trip since the group last met?

   • Have you found yourself thinking about or seeing particular experiences in your daily life differently as a result of your trip? If so, share examples.

2. Reflect back on your goals and obstacles from unit 8:

   • What has been going well?

   • What has been difficult?

3. In what areas would you like to grow, whether by incorporating a new goal or improving on a current goal?

4. How can your team pray for you as the Holy Spirit continues to work in your heart and as you seek to engage more deeply with God's work in the world?

RESOURCE MODULE A: FUNDRAISING

Pursuing a trip focused on long-term engagement, learning, fellow-ship, and encouragement should also impact how we fund our trips. Given the incredible amount of financial resources invested in a trip, we have a responsibility to communicate to donors what the trip will be and how we are committed to making the trip worth the financial investment. To that end, here are some general principles for raising support:

- You need to personally contribute to the cost of your trip. In the same way that the materially poor are more likely to "own" their own poverty alleviation and improvement if they have a personal and financial stake in the activities, you are more likely to steward this opportunity well if you have invested your own hard-earned cash in the trip. Your leader will work with you to determine what level of personal investment will be appropriate.

- You need to be realistic with your supporters about what you will be doing on this trip and what you won't be doing. Recognize that the trip costs significant financial resources, and make it clear how you plan to make their investment count over the long-term.

- Use this as an opportunity to advocate for the ministry you are visiting. Highlight the long-term work they are doing and how God is already at work through them. Make it clear that the purpose of this trip is to come alongside them.

Consider the following sample fundraising letter:

Dear _____,

I hope you are well, and that you are enjoying the onset of spring. As someone who has invested so much in me over the years, I wanted to let you know about an opportunity I have this summer.

A small group of people from my church, Deer Creek Church, has committed to an eight- to ten-month process of learning about poverty and appropriate poverty alleviation strategies. This involves fully participating in two months of preparatory meetings, a one-week trip, and multiple meetings over six to eight months after the trip. We will be traveling to Philadelphia, PA from July 10–July 17 to be with our brothers and sisters at Peace Fellowship Church. For the past fifteen years, PFC has been actively involved in ministry and poverty alleviation in its community. They started by working with local schools to support and staff after-school tutoring programs, developing relationships with low-income students and their families. PFC's community was heavily impacted by the 2008 recession, which led to even higher unemployment rates. Thus, PFC has developed financial education and jobs preparedness ministries in its community, helping individuals and families support themselves and find dignity through work.

PFC recognizes that poverty is about more than just a lack of material things. They are digging deep into the community, developing relationships with neighborhood leaders and members and walking with them over time as they move out of poverty. I realize that I can't do in seven days what has taken them years to do. As a result, instead of focusing on completing particular projects, here are my goals for my time in Philadelphia:

- Exploring how God is calling me to engage with missions and poverty alleviation as I continue to grow.

- Assisting and supporting PFC in whatever way they desire while we are there.

- Spending time with PFC staff and the residents of their neighborhood, observing the work God is already doing in their community and learning from their experiences.

- Encouraging and fellowshiping with my brothers and sisters in Christ, learning how I can best pray for and support their work over time.

Would you please join me in praying for PFC, the community members, and the team of people from my church? Pray that God will continue to open up new avenues and opportunities for PFC to demonstrate the hope of the gospel, and that our team would be humble encouragers and supporters as we enter their community.

Further, would you pray about contributing to the financial requirements of this trip? I realize that asking you to invest your God-given resources in a trip focused on learning from and fellowshiping with community members may seem strange. However, I take your investment seriously. In fact, I am dedicating some of my own money to the cost of the trip. You see, I am committed to making this trip one piece of a process of learning and action. Along with my teammates, I will be exploring how to support, engage with, and foster effective ministry and poverty alleviation efforts like PFC's—whether in my own community or across the globe.

Please return the enclosed card if you would like to receive prayer updates before and after the trip. Further, if you would like to invest in this trip financially, please enclose a check to Deer Creek Church with my name and "PFC Trip" in the memo line. The total cost of the trip will be $600, which will include bus transportation, lodging, and most of my meals. If you choose to give financially, it would be helpful for planning purposes to have any contributions by May 15.

Thank you so much for your time and the many ways you have been a part of my life. I look forward to seeing what God has in store for this summer and beyond, and it is a privilege to have people like you come alongside me in that process.

In Christ,

Maria

RESOURCE MODULE B: CULTURAL NORMS

CULTURAL NORMS
Subconscious assumptions, behaviors, and protocols that people naturally follow without even thinking about them

Concept of Time: *What is time, and how is it to be used?*

• Monochronic Cultures: Time is a limited resource that must be used carefully, so you need to save time and not waste time. Punctuality and efficiency reign supreme.

• Polychronic Cultures: Time is nebulous and almost limitless. There is always more time, so relationships trump efficiency.

Concept of Time

MONOCHRONIC   POLYCHRONIC

US   Asia   Africa

Latin America

Adapted from Craig Storti, *Figuring Foreigners Out: A Practical Guide* (Yarmouth, ME: Intercultural Press, 1999), 82.

Concept of Self: *What is "self," and where does it find importance?*

• Individualistic Cultures: Identity is found in being unique, and success is "being all you can be" by exercising freedom of choice. Independence is a core value.

• Collectivist Cultures: Identity is found in being a part of a broader group and success is knowing and fulfilling your role in the group. Interdependence is a core value.

Concept of Self

INDIVIDUALIST   COLLECTIVIST

Adapted from Craig Storti, *Figuring Foreigners Out: A Practical Guide* (Yarmouth, ME: Intercultural Press, 1999), 52.

Face and Directness: *How do you respect others?*

- Low Face Cultures: Direct and open communication is more important than not causing someone embarrassment or preventing conflict. Not telling the truth is less socially acceptable than getting angry with someone.

- High Face Cultures: Protecting people's honor is very important. Indirect communication is preferred and seen as more mature. Actions or words that could cause shame or embarrassment to others are to be avoided. Getting angry with others is less socially acceptable than avoiding telling the truth if doing so will hurt someone.

Saving Face

FACE LESS IMPORTANT   FACE MORE IMPORTANT

Adapted from Craig Storti, *Figuring Foreigners Out: A Practical Guide* (Yarmouth, ME: Intercultural Press, 1999), 98.

Degree of Directness

DIRECT   INDIRECT

Adapted from Craig Storti, *Figuring Foreigners Out: A Practical Guide* (Yarmouth, ME: Intercultural Press, 1999), 99.

Locus of Control: *What change is possible?*

- Internal Locus of Control: People can control their lives and are responsible for overcoming challenges. All problems can and should be solved.

- External Locus of Control: Complex outside forces influence life and cannot be easily understood or overcome. People should accept most things in life as they can't really change them easily.

Locus of Control

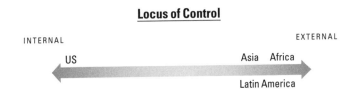

Adapted from Craig Storti, *Figuring Foreigners Out: A Practical Guide* (Yarmouth, ME: Intercultural Press, 1999), 82.

Power Distance: *How do you interact with authority?*

- Low Power Distance: People under authority are free to share their ideas and speak into the decision-making process. It is possible to disagree with authority in appropriate ways. People do not like to be micromanaged.

- High Power Distance: Authority figures are expected to use their power fully for the benefit of those under their authority. People should not disagree with authority. People like to be micromanaged.

Power Distance

Adapted from Craig Storti, *Figuring Foreigners Out: A Practical Guide* (Yarmouth, ME: Intercultural Press, 1999), 140.

NOTES

Unit 1

1. Robert J. Priest, "Short-Term Missions as a New Paradigm," in *Mission After Christendom: Emergent Themes in Contemporary Mission*, ed. Ogbu U. Kalu, Peter Vethanayagamony, and Edmund Kee-Fook Chia (Louisville, KY: Westminster John Knox Press, 2010), 86.

2. Robert Wuthnow, *Boundless Faith: The Global Outreach of American Churches* (Berkeley, CA: University of California Press, 2009), 171.

3. Robert J. Priest and Joseph Paul Priest, "'They See Everything and Understand Nothing': Short-Term Mission and Service Learning," *Missiology* 36, no. 1 (January 2008): 57.

4. Wuthnow, *Boundless Faith*, 180.

5. Ibid., 180.

6. Bryant L. Myers, *Walking with the Poor: Principles and Practices of Transformational Development* (Maryknoll, NY: Orbis Books, 1999), 86.

Unit 2

1. David A. Livermore, *Serving with Eyes Wide Open: Doing Short-Term Missions with Cultural Intelligence* (Grand Rapids, MI: Baker Publishing Group, 2006), 90–91.

Unit 3

1. This is a modification of the definition of paternalism found in Roland Bunch, *Two Ears of Corn: A Guide to People-Centered Agricultural Improvement* (Oklahoma City, OK: World Neighbors, 1982), 19–23.

Unit 4

1. Livermore, *Serving with Eyes Wide Open*, 95–96.

2. "Michael" and "Shelley," interview by Katie Casselberry, March 11, 2014.

3. Marco Perez, interview by Katie Casselberry, Lookout Mountain, GA, January 15, 2013.

4. "Jason," interview by Katie Casselberry, October 30, 2013.

Unit 5

1. Miriam Adeney, "The Myth of the Blank Slate: A Check List for Short-Term Missions," in *Effective Engagement in Short-Term Missions: Doing it Right!*, ed. Robert J. Priest (Pasadena, CA: William Carey Library, 2008), 132.

Unit 6

1. We are incredibly grateful for the input of Kurt Ver Beek, Jo Ann Van Engen, and David Livermore, whose comments influenced this unit, as well as units 7 and 8.

2. The questions in this section also reflect insights from "Michael" and "Shelley," interview.

Unit 8

1. Priest and Priest, "'They See Everything and Understand Nothing,'" 57.

2. Dennis Horton, Sarah Caldwell, Rachel Calhoun, Josh Flores, Chris Gerac, and Gabrielle Leonard, "Short-Term Mission Trips: What the Long-Term Mission Personnel Really Think about Them," *The Year 2013 Annual Proceedings of the ASSR*, ed. Jon K. Loessin and Scott Stripling (2013): 71.

ACKNOWLEDGMENTS

This project is a result of the encouragement and work of countless people, including:

Katie Casselberry, who shepherded this project from start to finish, using her vast skills at research, writing, and organization. Without Katie's commitment, dedication, and perseverance, this project would never have been completed.

Andy Jones of the Chalmers Center and our team at Moody Publishers, including Duane Sherman, Pam Pugh, and Parker Hathaway, who worked tirelessly to bring this project to fruition.

David Livermore, Jo Ann Van Engen, and Kurt Ver Beek, who graciously reviewed several units of this project and shared their insights and experiences with us. Thank you for your collaboration and encouragement.

The many church and ministry leaders who shared their wisdom, perspectives, and stories with us as we crafted the written manuscript, including Ron Barnes, Gregg Burgess, David Campbell, Scott Dewey, Jeff Galley, Opal Hardgrove, Sam Haupt, Shawn Janes, Kurt Kandler, Cathi Linch, Joel and Krista McCutcheon, Sam Moore, Marco Perez, Donald Thompson, Greg and Bobbi Van Schoyck, and James Ward.

John Holberg and Callie Dixon, who contributed to the research and revision process. Thank you for being so generous with your time and gifts.

The team at RightNow Media, especially Justin Forman, Phil Warner, Mark Blitch, and Mark Weaver, who crafted the videos that accompany this project.

The 410 Bridge, Mercy Ministries, Sunshine Gospel Ministries, Videre, and the countless people who coordinated and participated in interviews for the video units: Scott and Melanie Dewey, Crizauld Francois, Jedlain Geffrard, Joel Hamernick, Kurt Kandler, Diane

Pulvermiller, James Ward, and many others.

The teams from North Point Church, 12Stone Church, and Hixson Presbyterian Church, who graciously allowed us to film their visits in Haiti and Chicago. Thanks for allowing us to join you and share your reflections.

All the pastors and church leaders we have met who are trying to mobilize their congregations to advance Christ's kingdom, including Juan Constantino, Patrick Dominguez, Steve Daugherty, Sarah Frank, Jeff Galley, Bobby Griffith, David Hardin, Scott Harris, Jeff Jernigan, Gretchen Kerr, Johnny Long, Mary McClear, Andy Merrick, Mike Miller, Maria Penzes, Jeff Redding, Tim Ritter, Ray Sanabria, Chris Seaton, Doug Serven, Jason Surratt, Mark Swarner, Marcia Trani, Lorena Valle, Scott Wiggins, Barry Wilks, and countless others.

I (Steve) was so blessed by the support of my amazing partner and wife Mary, my seven kids and two sons-in-law, my church, and my Covenant College students. They all prayed for me and encouraged me as I worked on this project and completed my teaching responsibilities.

I (Brian) want to thank my wonderful wife, Jill, and my three fantastic children for their enduring support and encouragement of my work with the Chalmers Center, including this project. As important as this work is to me, it pales in comparison to them.

As always, all praise and glory to God for His continual grace and mercy in our lives. Jesus Christ's power to make all things new, both in our lives and in the world through His church, is our only hope and salvation.

—Steve Corbett and Brian Fikkert

 The
Chalmers
Center

YOU DON'T
HAVE TO TRAVEL
HUNDREDS OF MILES.

Empower the
poor in your
own backyard.

Faith & Finances:
Church-centered
financial education
and discipleship

Get Trained. **www.chalmers.org/train**

The
Chalmers
Center

YOUR STORY
ISN'T OVER YET.

Learn more
about how
to walk with
the poor...

Engaging in
your community
and around
the world...

Leading to
lasting change
in their lives—
and yours.

Find more resources at **www.chalmers.org**